Rice
Lake

Lake Amelia L.

Minnehaha Falls

Mud Lake

Wm. G. Gilmore

George Stewart

Aaron Hoover
400 a.

P. Christian

A. Scott

John Goudie

Cedar Ave.

Post Rd.

34TH Ave.

Publication Notes

Text, Image Selection, and Project Design

Deborah Morse-Kahn, Regional Research Associates, Minneapolis

Book Design, Typesetting, and Production Management

Bolger, Concept to Print, Minneapolis

ISBN: 0-9605054-1-5

Chapters in the City History

Edina

By Deborah Morse-Kahn

Dedication

This book is a gift from the City of Edina to Ken Rosland for forty-four years of generous, progressive and thoughtful leadership:

Park and Recreation Aide 1955
Assistant Parks Director 1958-1962
Park Director 1962-1977
City Manager 1977-1998

Appreciations

First thanks must go to the Edina Historical Society's staff, volunteers and board of directors: they put up with major chaos as every drawer, cabinet, and box in the archives was turned out to support the research of this book. Most importantly, over the past years they patiently helped me to catalogue hundreds of new photographs into the existing collections: without such practical familiarity with the city's photo imagery, this book would have been inconceivable.

I sought and received the invaluable advice and companionship of many friends and colleagues in the community: Ken Rosland, Ralph Campbell, Joyce Repya, Bob Kojetin, and everyone at the City of Edina who believed so strongly in this project; Debbie Miller and David Nystuen at the Minnesota Historical Society who, in their unique and wonderful ways, brought me into the proper mindset and humor for such a monumental undertaking, and Tracey Baker, Jon Walstrom, Ruth Bauer, and Scott Anfinson of the same institution for invaluable referrals to materials and resources; Ed Kukla, Jo Ellen Haugo and all the special collections staff at the Minneapolis Collection of the Minneapolis Public Library who dug countless dusty files out of cabinets for my perusal; Jack Kabrud, curator of the Hennepin History Museum without whose support, good cheer and friendship I would have flagged long ago; and Barbara Bezat of the Northwest Architectural Archives of the University of Minnesota for always responding to my calls with patience, knowledge, and affection.

Thank you all. After these many years of working with, for, and around each other, the pleasure is still mine.

The directors of the Richfield Historical Society, the Bloomington Historical Society, the Eden Prairie Historical Society, the St. Louis Park Historical Society, the Hopkins Historical Society, and the Western Hennepin County Pioneers Association gave generously of their time and made available to me on several instances photographic imagery exclusive to their collections.

The author wishes to thank the City of Edina for permission to quote from city publications, including *History of Edina, Minnesota* (Hesterman) and *From the Barber's Chair* (Swanson and Clark), and to adapt previously published material written by the author for the city's quarterly *About Town*.

Barbara Wehr Bergan of Edina provided a bright and shining presence at the exact moment that I needed inspiration for a best approach to writing the history of Edina. Barby, I was so lucky to meet you when I did. Thank you for all you gave to this effort and I hope you are pleased with the result.

David Lanegran, Professor of Geography at St. Paul's Macalester College—and the true dean of local history studies in the Twin Cities metropolitan community—shared insights, anecdotes, and considerations of theories and successes in researching and writing local history: I was, and remain, humbled and immensely appreciative, not least for the reminder that my Master's Degree confers only a piece of paper, not knowledge. Education is forever.

The bright, gifted and consistently professional project team at Bolger—Tom Radant, Susan Bennett, and Becky Pfluger—played a critically important role in the design and production of this book. I could not have managed without them; that we became such great friends in the process was an unlooked-for gift.

The heart and happiness for my work comes from the support of the many friends and extended family who have been with me all along this journey to a writing life in American historic studies, who stay with me for the love of the work and for wanting, as I do, an illumination of our collective community history, lest we forget the breathtaking detail of the labor and the joys and the worries and the great, grand times that have passed our way. You know who you are, and you know how I feel, and I am so grateful.

Deborah Morse-Kahn
Summer 1998

Considerations

This book is a pictorial study, a collection of detailed visual images matched to essays discussing the life and times of historic Richfield Township and of Edina, one of two communities that evolved from the earlier territorial designation.

All told, with the addition of photographs from other local historical societies, the Minnesota Historical Society, and the Hennepin County Museum, some 3,500 images were considered and reviewed for inclusion in this book.

A substantial gift of research and resources had, in the last 20 years, been made available to the City of Edina in the form of three excellent publications: Paul Hesterman's *History of Edina, Minnesota* (1988), William Scott & Jeffrey Hess' *History and Architecture of Edina, Minnesota* (1981), and Vern Swanson and Tom Clark's *From the Barber's Chair: 50th and France 1936-1988.* The existence of these thoughtful and detailed studies of Edina permitted me the luxury of creating a broad photographic essay wrapped in words, knowing that the year-by-year, name-by-name, street-by-street historical summaries of the city had already been well realized.

My work then, as I saw it, was to illuminate for the pioneer Edina resident, and for the newcomer as well, significant chapters in the community history. Writing a local history can be devilishly difficult—what to include? And how much? To what extent are individuals or single families to be extolled? Should one work for a comprehensive history, or opt instead for moments in time?

The City of Edina has been many things: a traditional homeland over countless hundreds of years for nomadic Dakota tribal families; a Civil War mill crossroads on a creek; a village for prosperous Quaker farmers and, through them, also home for one of Minnesota's Black pioneering communities; a village of Irish Catholic farmers; host to one of the state's principal and most active Grange fellowships; the home of not one but three nationally known livestock farms; the first Minneapolis suburb to see a streetcar line extended through its boundaries; the unexpected host to one of the most exclusive, costly and elegant residential districts in the nation; home to an ingenious experiment in all-enclosed climate-controlled retailing that would influence architects and merchants around the country for the next forty years, culminating in the development of the world's largest shopping mall.

That Edina is unique in the nation is unchallenged. It is home to one of the highest per capita income communities in the country while quietly and respectfully caring for citizens well familiar with the poverty line. It is home to one of the most thoughtfully designed urban green space and parks programs in the metropolitan nine-county region, this at a time when property values have steadily moved to the stratosphere. It is a comfortable home to over twenty-five distinct ethnic subcommunities making up its citizenry in the 1990s.

Far from common, never homogenous, only the mythologies about Edina have remained monolithic, and those mythologies are largely out of recent collective memory that recalls only the prosperous post-war years of this extraordinary city. The challenge to this regional historian was obvious, and the pressure immense, not least being the need to ensure that my abiding respect and affection for this community not interfere with my objectivity in relating their story. Not all the chapters were pretty ones.

I have opted, then, to illuminate the collective community history in favor of the individual story except in those instances where the actions of a few became of critical significance beyond the borders of the village. This was not an easy choice: many may feel slighted, some old pioneer family names may have been neglected, buildings of architectural significance left unreferenced. I hope that the earlier studies of Edina mentioned above, which did such a thorough job of detailing the life of the individual person and place, will be of continuing pleasure and comfort.

One nagging question remained: at what decade or era of community development should the book come to a close? An easy choice, seemingly, at first consideration, for the city's centennial was in 1988, a logical place to conclude. Yet, after months of handling the vast photo imagery available for inclusion in this book, it was clear that after the 1960s with the sudden popularity of inexpensive cameras, photo images began to change both in form and appearance, so much so that one could draw a clear demarcation line between the last of the 'Brownie Camera' black-and-white scallop-edged snapshots of our 1950s family albums and the sudden rise of the color polaroid in the late 1960s. Because the rise of popular photography generated immense numbers of pictures after the 1960s that are easily available to all of us, the decision among the publishing team convened to design this book was to stop in 1965.

We hope that this book, a deeply satisfying and hugely challenging project, pleases you as much as it pleases us, and that it will prove both entertaining and illuminating.

v

Table of Contents

Dedication i

Appreciations i

Considerations iii

Chapter 1: One Hundred & Fifty Years 1

Chapter 2: A Crossroads in Time 11

Chapter 3: The Mill on the Creek 25

Chapter 4: Baird, Brown, Bull & Grimes 35

Chapter 5: The Black Pioneers 53

Chapter 6: At the Turn of the Century 63

Chapter 7: Morningside & the Country Club District 83

Chapter 8: Modern Times 99

Chapter 9: Edina in the War Years 117

Chapter 10: Southdale 131

Chapter 11: Postwar to Centennial: The Boom Years 141

National Register Properties in Edina 161

About the Author 161

Research Notes 162

Chapter 1

Sometimes when I drive home at night on Highway 62 and see the lights of Southdale and all those houses I can't help but think how things have changed. Why, I can remember building sand castles in the middle of France Avenue when I was a little girl. We had about thirty-two acres of land off France Avenue. We raised vegetables for the wholesale houses in Minneapolis—parsley, carrots, cauliflower, green beans. Between France and Beard Avenues, and between 60th and 62nd Street, there was nothing but a large hayfield..."

As remembered by Aldora Cornelius Hallaway, who grew up in a farmhouse at 6101 France Avenue South (now razed). From Scott & Hess, *History and Architecture of Edina, Minnesota*, 1979

The John Tierney farm near West 60th Street at the Edina-Minneapolis-Richfield borders, 1954.

Richfield Historical Society

3

J.A. (Sonny) Danens & Sons putting up hay in the Village of Edina, ca. 1930s. The Danens were every-where in Edina village life, working with their popular horse team in the truck farm fields, grooming the Country Club District lots during a decade of development, and excavating many of the new residential and commercial foundations throughout the village.

Edina Historical Society

In 1959, a century after the first Edina settlers had staked their farms in historic western Richfield Township, the farm of James and Lydia Green ceased production. It had anchored southern Edina at the lower end of Cahill Road since the turn of the century and was the last operating farm in the city limits.

In the decades to follow, the Greens' farm faced the encroachment of modern development: a shopping center, apartment buildings, industrial plants, hotels. James Green died in 1972 and Lydia and their son Foster stayed on, boarding horses in the aged three-story wooden barn. Wooden-wheeled carts, long unused, slept under the trees.

And when the Greens' property was finally sold and re-zoned by the city for the Dewey Hill Condominiums in 1985, the farmsite destruction by burning in a fire department exercise marked the end of the last farm in the City of Edina, fittingly in the Cahill District, a Civil War-era farming crossroads and the oldest settlement site in the city.

It might seem strange in the 1990s to consider Edina as a farming community, yet the modern developments of Southdale Shopping Center, the schools, the Edina Country Club and residential district, the Interlachen Country Club, Braemar Park, all were built on the sizable acreages of family farms sold for land development.

The Willson children on the family farm to the southwest of present-day Highway 100 and West 50th Street, south of the old Eden Prairie Road, ca. 1880. The road running the western border of the Edina Country Club golf course now bears the family name.

Edina Historical Society

5

Some of the early Edina farms were as large as 400 and 500 acres but the quarter-section farm of 160 acres was most common in Edina. Smaller farms of forty and eighty acres were certainly frequent, tucked in here and there amidst their greater neighbors.

Grain farming was the norm for the larger holdings—wheat, corn and oats and speciality livestock put several Edina farms on the national map: Baird sheep—Spanish Merino, English Cotswold, Shropshire, Lincoln—were consistent prize-winners and the Browndale farm reached world fame (and world-class prices) by the turn of the century in its cattle and horses. Most, though, were small berry and truck farms scattered throughout the village and managed handily by single families or several generations on adjacent holdings.

After Edina's incorporation in 1888, new ordinances were written to manage life within a rural farming community, providing variously for the location and licensing of slaughterhouses and stockyards, for the disposal of animal waste, for the restriction of fast driving of horses within the village limits, and to deal with livestock when they became a nuisance.

The mid-'20s saw many regulations that were pointers to an increasing suburbanization of a rural district: farming had been declining since the turn of the century, dropping from 166 farms in 1895 to seventy-five farms in 1925. The village was becoming a city.

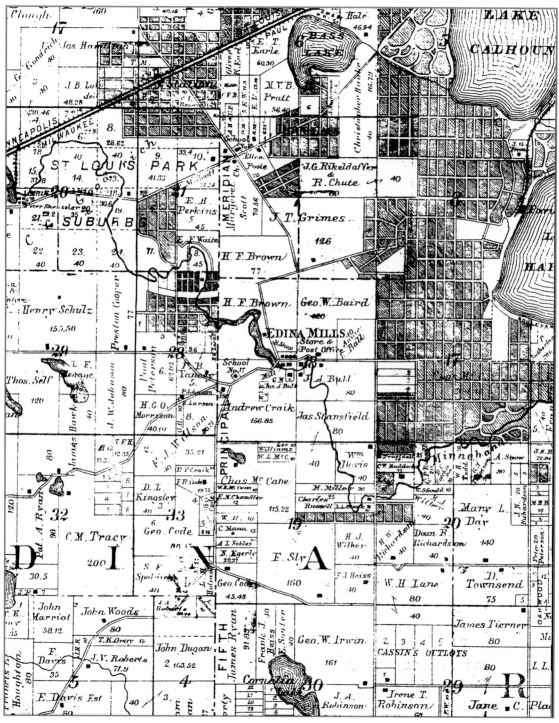

The Village of Edina Mills, 1890.

Peter K. Johnson and daughter, ca. 1915, on their small farm tucked in the triangle formed by present-day Highway 100 and the old Eden Prairie Road.

Cahill

"*Each morning we were usually awakened at about 5:00 a.m. by the shrill cry of a rooster. We would get up, feed the animals, milk about thirty or forty cows, clean out the barn and get ourselves ready for breakfast. This frequently consisted of fried potatoes, fried eggs, fried salt pork, homemade bread, rolls, butter, milk and coffee, and a cooked cereal with lots of cream. After breakfast I had about a mile to walk to school...*"

From *School Days at Cahill* by Thomas J. (Joe) Ryan, 1975, Age 99

By 1930, hastened by the availability of the automobile and convenient streetcar access, the farm fields of the Bairds and the Browns had been built over by Thorpe Bros. Country Club development, and the old Edina Mill torn down in 1933. The elegant new developments of Rolling Green, Mirror Lakes, and Edina Highlands swallowed more farms in the postwar '40s and ground was broken for the smaller districts of White Oaks, South Harriet Park, and Brucewood. By the end of the Second World War the old cartroads had been paved, all traces of the early cowpaths were gone, the creamery in downtown Edina closed, and the city livestock pound no longer required.

The Southdale Shopping Center was built on the Day-Roberts farms in the mid-1950s and Braemar Park consumed the 414 acres of the old Hayes farm in 1959, by which time Edina had been ranked fourth in development pace among Minneapolis suburbs. By 1960, all city streets were being expanded and improved and major highways were being routed through and around the city.

When the horses were led for the last time from the Greens' barn in 1973, a quarter-century of building and development had swept past the inheritance of a rural farming community and relegated those quieter days to the history books.

The James & Lydia Green Farm, ca. 1965, once located at present-day Cahill Road and West 70th Street, was the last operating farm in Edina, razed in 1985 to make way for residential development.

Edina Historical Society

Many of Edina's agricultural holdings in the northern districts were small truck farms while in the southern areas much larger grain farm holdings were the norm. This pattern persisted well into the 1950s until the planning of the metropolitan area freeways spelled the end of first-tier suburban farms.

Edina's truck farmers raised vegetables and berry crops to sell at the Minneapolis markets, keeping a few cows, some chickens, perhaps ducks for family needs. Beekeeping was also common and the honey, along with hens' eggs, was a commonly sold commodity at roadside stands and at the city markets.

10

Feeding the chickens on an Edina farm, ca. 1930.

Chapter 2

*T*he Land Office at Minneapolis' Bridge Square was the scene of steady business in the 1850s and 1860s and the prospective landowners moved out south, west and north from the fledgling town and from St. Anthony across the river to mark off and build on their new acreages...The part of the Fort Snelling Reserve soon to be called Richfield Township was formed below the town of Minneapolis and stretched from the Mississippi River west to the source of Nine Mile Creek, and included most of Minnehaha Creek as well...

11

The Falls of St. Anthony, ca. 1865. The falls were the site of the earliest government mills at St. Anthony and its neighboring town Minneapolis. Both towns grew rapidly with steady commerce and available land.

Minnesota Historical Society

A Crossroads in Time

Stubbs

Lura Bridges Butterfield (Holman), 1814-1904, grandmother of Lura Ellen Butterfield Stubbs, Edina Mills.

"I was born October 8, 1883 on a farm at Edina. My father was Frank Butterfield and my mother Sarah Roberts Butterfield. The house has long since been gone. Frank Butterfield's farm…was in Section 33 of old Richfield [Township] but was in Edina when it was incorporated out of Richfield on December 18, 1888."

Lura Ellen Butterfield Stubbs,
Minnesota Memories: 1887-1917

"Indians Traveling" was painted by Captain Seth Eastman out of Fort Snelling at the confluence of the Minnesota (St. Peter) and Mississippi Rivers in 1850.

Minnesota Historical Society

In the Minnesota Territory

Samuel and Gideon Pond established their mission in 1834 on the shore of Lake Calhoun in the wild lands southwest of the fledgling river towns of St. Anthony and Minneapolis. Cloud Man (Marpiya-wichasta) and his people were farming there to satisfy Fort Snelling's hope that raising subsistence crops would be a better life for the ever-pressed Dakota Nation than nomadic hunting and fishing on shrinking homelands.

The Pond's mission and school was not the first attempt to proselytize the Christian religion and a European lifestyle to the Dakota Nation, but what was exceptional was that the Ponds worked to understand the tribal peoples of the Minnesota River Valley, studying Dakota religion and customs and language. There was a charitable peace between the Minnesota tribal communities and the mission up on the river heights. The Pond's diaries gave Minnesota an exceptionally detailed written record of Dakota life in the 1800s at the time of the re-establishment of the permanent mission site further south on the Minnesota River, at Oak Grove in Bloomington.

At the time of the creation of the State of Minnesota in 1858, the Minnesota Valley's six Mdewakanton (People of Spirit Lake) Dakota tribal peoples—those of the villages of Chiefs Shakopee, Wabasha, Wacouta, Little Crow, Black Dog, and Pennesha—had been removed

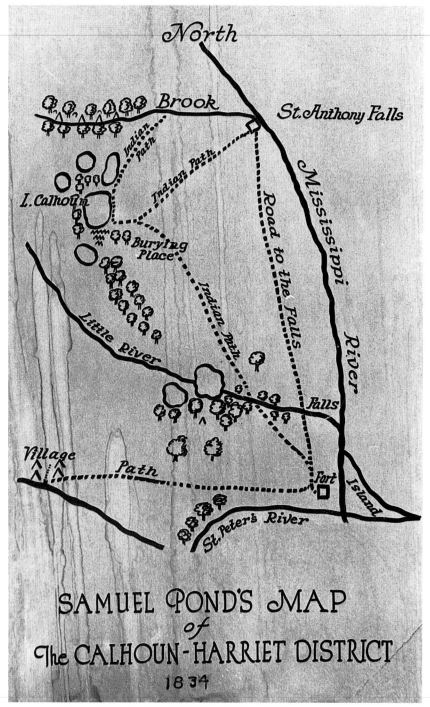

North

Brook

St. Anthony Falls

Indian Path

Indian Path

Mississippi River

L. Calhoun

Burying Place

Road to the Falls

Indian Path

Little River

Falls

Village

Path

Fort

Island

St. Peter's River

SAMUEL POND'S MAP
of
The CALHOUN-HARRIET DISTRICT
1834

This realization of a hand-drawn map by Samuel Pond, one of two missionary brothers to the Dakota in the early 1800s, depicts the paths out of the Fort Snelling Reserve to the vital destinations of St. Anthony, Cloudman's village and tribal burying ground at Lake Calhoun, and Dakota villages west along the Minnesota (St. Peter) River. The 'Brook' at the north is most likely present-day Bassett's Creek. The 'Little River' at the mid-point of the map is today's Minnehaha Creek.

Minnesota Historical Society

to the lands of Fort Ridgely up the river near Redwood Falls. In 1862, after a year of forced starvation and imprisonment, the despair and rage of the Dakota leaders over the plight of their children overwhelmed the Minnesota River valley and resulted in the deaths of many area settlers and the eventual execution of the Dakota accused at Fort Snelling. Reservation life became a permanent Dakota reality.

The dwindling of the Dakota nation to reservation life and solitary nomadic travels took them to the background of the land boom taking place in the Minnesota Territory. The Land Office at Minneapolis' Bridge Square was the scene of steady business and the prospective landowners moved out south,

The Edina Mill, ca. 1890, one of many small flouring mills to be built during and after the Civil War along Minnehaha creek between Lake Minnetonka's Grays Bay and Minnehaha Falls.

Edina Historical Society

west and north from the fledgling town and from St. Anthony across the river to mark off and build on their new acreages.

The part of the Fort Snelling Reserve soon to be called Richfield Township was formed below the town of Minneapolis and stretched from the Mississippi River west to the source of Nine Mile Creek, and included most of Minnehaha Creek as well. The eastern half (later Richfield) was flat lands and rich soil. The western half (later Edina) was far less of either, being part of what had been known as 'The Big Woods.' Once heavily forested with elm, maple, bass and oak, the district after clearance soon earned the name 'Hard Scrabble Hills' for the resulting undulating rock-strewn landscape.

Despite these aspects, the region was close to both the Fort and the market centers of Minneapolis and St. Anthony, promised abundant timber and wild hay, and—most promising of all—held swift-flowing creeks that could supply milling power. By the year 1854 the entirety of Richfield Township had been claimed or preempted at the cost of $1.50 an acre and at the time of the Civil War, in 1860, showed a census population of 169 households.

The Cahill Settlement & the Edina Mill

By the year 1870 there were seventeen Irish families, refugees of the Irish potato famine, who had settled along a small area of Nine

The Roberts farmhouse stood on the old territorial Valley View Road just over the eastern boundary of Eden Prairie and a bit to the north of present-day Braemar Park in Edina. The farmhouse and springhouse were razed in 1963.

Edina Historical Society

Farmhouse

"The house and farm buildings were on the southwest corner of Nine Mile Creek where it passes under Valley View Road. A never-failing spring sent cold water through the spring-house…for over 100 years there was no well on the farm. Valley View was a main trail for Indians from the Shakopee colony [on the Minnesota River], and early settlers were also refreshed at the spring and at the public watering trough beside the creek…"

Roberts Family Letters, Edina Mills, Richfield Township, 1874

Mile Creek in western Richfield Township. The district would come to be called 'Cahill' to honor the Reverend F. Cahill who was serving as a Catholic missionary in southeastern Minnesota.

The Cahill families were farmers and their names—Delaney (who built the first house in what became Edina in 1854), Ryan, Kyte, McCauley, O'Meara, Maloney, Moriarty, Fogarty, Gleeson, McCabe, Duggan, Slavin— would dominate life in the south half of Edina for one hundred years. The Cahill Irish built a one-room school in 1864 which also served the community for village elections, dances and parties, plays and lectures. St. Patrick's Church had long existed, first as a

log cabin in the 1840s near present-day Highway 100 and West 70th Street, then as three ever-larger incarnations to accommodate a burgeoning congregation. Though German and English farming families would later follow to the district, the Cahill Irish would endure as a social force well into the third and fourth generations.

In the far north of Richfield Township, on Minnehaha Creek, the Edina (Waterville) Mill was established. Though it passed through varying ownership in less than a decade, the mill proved to be the stabilizing economic force in the small community and, in time, made the development of the entire village possible.

Dakota and Ojibwe tipis could be seen regularly along the banks of the Mississippi River around the Nicollet, Hennepin and Spirit Islands district between St. Anthony and Minneapolis. These tipis were pitched on the river bank below Bridge Square in Minneapolis, 1854.

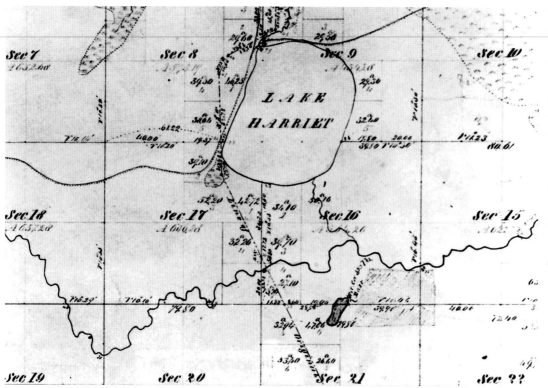

Edina Mills, as the district came to be known, was settled primarily by New Englanders—Quakers and Episcopalians and Presbyterians—whose progressive take on farming, civic life, and education would influence life for many well beyond the borders of their small village. Here were the Grimes, Baird, Willson, Bull, Craik, Millam, Cooper and Brown families, as well as the pioneer Black families—the Yanceys, Siggers, and Gillespies—who had come north from Tennessee after the Civil War to establish small berry farms and build a reputation for active civic participation that would endure in the village beyond the First World War.

The first village school built just prior to the Cahill School, had been established equidistant between the Cahill Settlement and Edina Mills at Code's Corner, named for the families that settled in the general area near present-day Normandale and Valley View Roads. This small school was moved to the mill crossroads in 1872 and, by the mid-1880s, the three other one-room schools—Cahill, Prattville (on Wooddale at Excelsior Boulevard) and Burnes (at the northwest corner of the Township on the Hopkins border)—were drawing ever-larger student enrollments. Such was the population pace that the decision was made to build a new two-story brick Edina School near the new village center at the mill district.

The Burnes School, 1880s, at Edina's northwest border with Hopkins, one of several one-room schoolhouses in neighboring villages that enrolled students from Edina.

Hopkins Historical Society

The Edina Grange

In 1866, Oliver Hudson Kelly of Elk River, Minnesota established the National Order of Patrons of Husbandry, soon to be known simply as 'The Grange.' The first State Grange in the Union was organized in St. Paul, Minnesota on February 23, 1869 and, out of an eventual total of forty-nine national granges, forty were in the state of Minnesota.

The Grange Society was the only national organization established to identify and solve issues of rural life and farming, which was one of the leading professions in the latter part of the nineteenth century. It was a fraternal organization, an educational institution, a cooperative business and a force for social betterment.

The fundamental purpose of The Grange was to make those living in a farm community happier, able to live a healthier life and become prosperous. The Grange worked in conjunction with the local churches, schools and other civic organizations that sought a better life and better government, fighting against intemperance, injustice, intolerance, extravagance, monopoly, graft and dishonesty.

The camaraderie of the Grange was particularly helpful for women. Most farming women had little opportunity for interaction with others beyond their own farms. The meetings and eventual friendships helped break up the isolation of farm life in a rural community, promoted self-confidence and instilled a sense

Cowperthwait's Map of the Minnesota Territory, 1850. The Mississippi River is easily traced from the lower right-hand corner up through the mid-section of the territory. The Falls and City of St. Anthony, Fort Snelling, and Mendota are clearly detailed, but note the absence of Minneapolis or any depiction of Lake Minnetonka, a sacred site carefully hidden from early surveyors for nearly a half-century after the establishment of the Fort Snelling Reserve.

of goodwill among its members. Women were not only invited to be members of the Grange, they were encouraged to participate in meetings and came to hold critical positions of leadership in the ensuing decades.

The Minnehaha Grange No. 398 was organized at Edina Mills in 1873 by George Baird and James A. Bull, reflecting the progressive agricultural movement fostered by Edina Mills' farm families. Initial membership in the new Minnehaha Grange came from Edina Mills, Richfield Mills, St. Louis Park, and Hopkins farm families, with membership swelling dramatically after the first year as Grange concepts and programs reached out to the southwestern Hennepin County farming community.

After the first anniversary of organization, members of the Minnehaha Grange distributed their own newsletter called the 'Minnehaha Spray' and made plans for the building of a new hall, raising the $400 needed through the incorporation of the Grange Association in 1879. The first meeting in the new hall, built at the corner of West 50th Street and Wood-dale Avenue, was held February 27, 1880 and the Grange, like the Cahill School at the south end of the village, became the critical gathering site for the social, educational, and civic affairs of the village.

And such a gathering site would have been critically necessary in 1888, for the split of Richfield Township, in great debate over

St. Louis Park's Prattville School, ca. 1890, another one-room schoolhouse well attended by children from the neighboring community of Edina Mills. In all, four one-room schoolhouses—Burnes (Hopkins), Prattville, Bush Lake (Bloomington), and Cahill—enrolled Edina pupils until a larger school could be built near the village's historic milling crossroads.

Edina Historical Society

encroaching urbanization, became a reality in that year and the western half of the old township—containing the Cahill district, the Mills crossroads, and Codes' Corner—took on the formal designation of 'village' and accorded itself the new name of 'Edina.'

RICHFIELD — 1874

From a Map of Hennepin County, Minnesota
Compiled by Geo. B. Wright, U.S. Surveyor
Published by Wright & Rice, Minneapolis

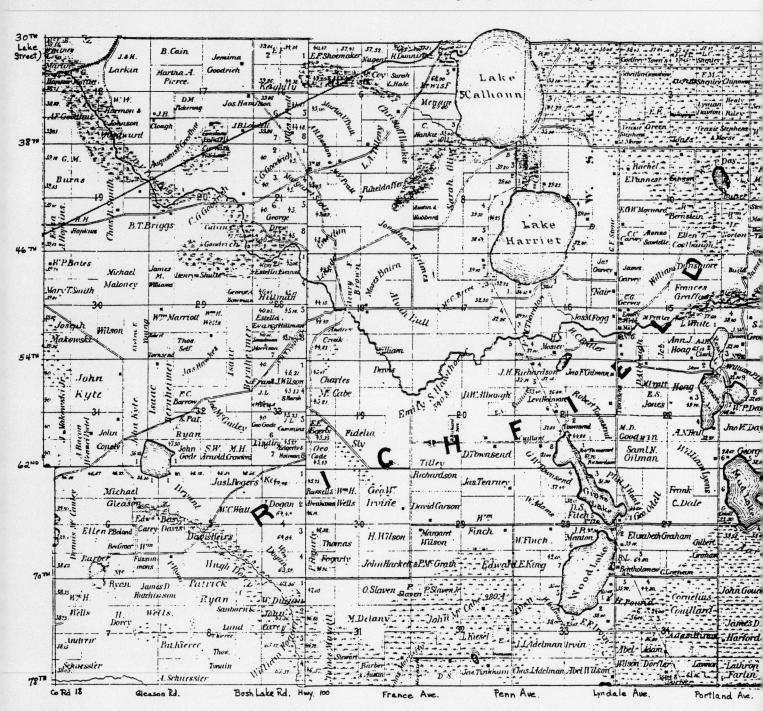

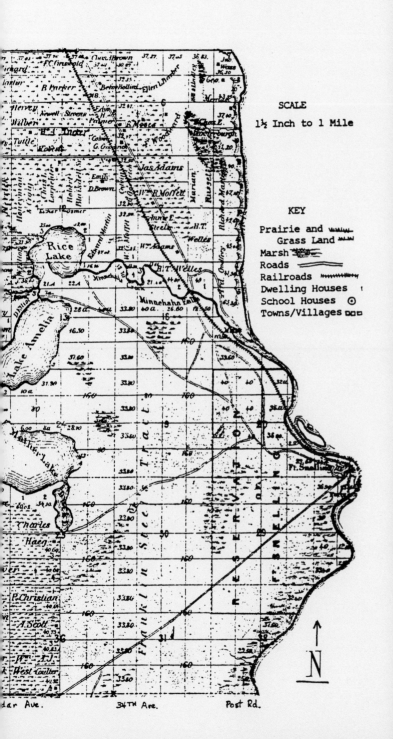

SCALE

1½ Inch to 1 Mile

KEY

Prairie and 〰〰
        Grass Land 〰〰
Marsh ≈≈
Roads ═══
Railroads ╬╬╬╬╬╬
Dwelling Houses ₁
School Houses ⊙
Towns/Villages ▭▭▭

N

The eastern half (later Richfield) was flat lands and rich soil. The western half (later Edina) was far less of either, being part of what had been known as 'The Big Woods.' Once heavily forested with elm, maple, bass and oak, the district after clearance soon earned the name 'Hard Scrabble Hills' for the resulting undulating rock-strewn landscape...

24

Richfield Township, 1874. The territorial district was eventually divided into two separate communities, Richfield and Edina, organizing in response to annexation pressures from the growing city of Minneapolis.

Richfield Historical Society

Chapter 3

*I*n the time of the Civil War, from 1861 to 1864, the mill ran day and night to meet requisitions from Fort Snelling and scouts were sent out into the countryside to scour farms for enough wheat to meet the quotas. [Jonathan] Grimes...with one of the first teams of horses in the district, made the delivery runs to the Fort, leaving again with an empty wagon and falling asleep, content to let the horses find their way home along the well-known road west...

At the crossroads of Edina Mills, ca. 1880.

Edina Historical Society

The Mill on the Creek

George Millam, ca. 1928, in the historic Edina Mill a few years before it was razed. Millam, a Scottish immigrant to the Minnesota Territory, had served as miller in Edina for several owners from 1869 to the late 1880s.

Edina Historical Society

The Edina Mill was one of six flour and timber mills that flourished in the second half of the 19th century along the run of Minnehaha Creek from its westernmost source near Grays Bay, Lake Minnetonka, to its mouth at the Mississippi River. In succession, from west to east, stood the Minnetonka Mill (1853), St. Alban's Mill (1874) in Hopkins, the Globe-Schussler Mill (1874) in St. Louis Park, the Waterville (Edina) Mill (1857, the Richfield Mill (1855), and the Godfrey Mill (1853) in Minneapolis at the mouth of Minnehaha creek on the Mississippi River.

The land on which the Waterville (Edina) Mill was built was pre-empted in 1855 by William Hoyt, who sold it a year later to the partnership of Jacob Elliott, Richard Strout, Levi Stewart, and Joseph Cushman. Richard Strout platted the town of Waterville in 1857 and a flouring mill was built on the stream that same year. John Stoopes was the first mill-wright and John Merriott was carpenter (and was said to have received a cow for payment).

The mill was sold once more in 1859 to Jonathan Grimes and William C. Rheem who upgraded the dam and access road. Grimes soon bought out his partner and, from his nearby farm, oversaw the village milling operations.

In the time of the Civil War, from 1861 to 1864, the mill ran day and night to meet requisitions from Fort Snelling and scouts were sent out into the countryside to scour farms

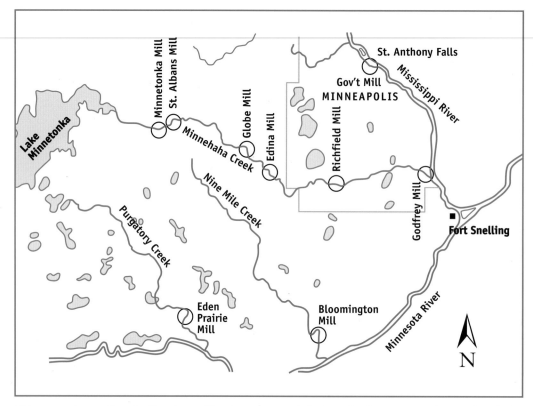

This map shows the six flouring mills that operated during the late 1800s along Minnehaha Creek, and several others in operation along Purgatory and Nine Mile Creeks in southwestern Hennepin County.

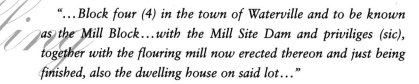

Milling

"…Block four (4) in the town of Waterville and to be known as the Mill Block…with the Mill Site Dam and priviliges (sic), together with the flouring mill now erected thereon and just being finished, also the dwelling house on said lot…"

Promissory Note, Levi M. Stewart, Richfield Township, July 1857.

for enough wheat to meet the quotas. Grimes, though not a miller by trade (he was a nurseryman) singlehandedly managed the complicated requisition accounts and, with one of the first teams of horses in the district, made most of the delivery runs to the Fort, leaving again with an empty wagon and, falling asleep, letting the horses find their way home along the well-known road west.

Grimes sold the mill to Daniel Buckwalter in 1867, who applied his own name to the mill. Changing hands—and names—again many times in the next several years, the site became known simply as the 'Red Mill' for the color it was painted.

Edina Mills

The mill was again purchased in 1869 by Andrew Craik, a Scots emigre via Canada who re-christened the mill 'Edina' from a poetic name from his native Edinburgh. The new name would eventually be adopted by the village at the time of its organization in 1888.

In Craik's day the millsite consisted of a two-story, rectangular building, forty feet long and thirty-six feet wide, of board-and-batten construction over a heavy timber partial-oak frame, with a gabled wood-shingled roof. Twelve-inch wide vertical planks covered the exterior walls. Two later additions were made in the form of small lean-to rooms on the

31

south and west sides of the building, most likely to house water-wheels. The mill was reached by road from the north along present-day Browndale Avenue and had a loading dock for the convenience of farmers. So steady was business that it was not uncommon to see twenty-five teams of oxen waiting at the mill at any one time.

Craik hired George Millam, also a Scot, to run the mill, expanded operations (and made Minnesota history) by specializing in pearl barley and oatmeal, creating a profitable market in Minneapolis. To process the barley and oats, Craik installed three turbine wheels furnishing fifty horsepower to three runs of

granite French burr (or 'buhr') millstones made of a special quartz quarried near Paris, France. Elevators were built to hold wheat and rye and a sandstone oat huller was added, as was a brick kiln to dry the oats.

Craik & Sons advertised oatmeal, pearl barley, flour, feed and grain, and milling at a profitable fee of a tenth of the milled proceeds. Grain was marketed at a feed store opened in Minneapolis at 126 Washington Avenue and managed by Craik's son, Alexander. Craik also built the district's first general store at the mill crossroads in 1869. The store was later operated by his son, John, and served as Edina Mills' first post office.

The abandoned mill, ca. 1930.

The patronage of the Cahill Irish from the southern end of the district was vital to the Edina Mills economy. The mill served as a convenient place for the Cahill families to have grain made into flour on the road up to Minneapolis. And farmers coming in from the neighboring districts of northwest Bloomington, Eden Prairie, St. Louis Park, and Hopkins also made use of the mill, as did the Dakota passing through on their way north from the Minnesota River.

Craik sold the mill to his employee, George Millam, in 1875, who sold it again 1889 to Henry F. Brown, owner of the adjacent Browndale Farm. Brown constructed an earthen dam to raise the water and improve flow to the milling operation, but water power became a continuing problem as the creek level fluctuated wildly. The final blow came in 1895 when the Grays Bay dam was constructed at the source of Minnehaha Creek where it flowed out of Lake Minnetonka. Brown finally shut down the mill—indeed, the Grays Bay dam spelled the end of all the Minnehaha Creek mills—and used the mill-house to store grain.

The Past

Thorpe Bros. Realtors bought the Browndale Farm and the Edina mill site in 1922 for the development of a new residential community, the Country Club District, and there was hope in the village that the old mill could be preserved as an historic site. Meetings were held but no progress made towards preservation. A final epitaph for the venerable structure— 'The Past'— was fashioned out of fieldstones by workmen clearing the old Browndale Farm across the road. In 1932, the old mill was finally torn down.

Workmen preparing to tear down the old mill for Thorpe Bros.' new Country Club District spell out 'The Past" in fieldstones (far right) beyond the old Browndale Farm gateposts, ca. 1928.

Minnesota Historical Society

The farmer of today must do something besides 'get up early' and work hard from early morn to dewy eve. There must be method, calculation, and intelligence in his operations, which necessitates that he be not the hayseed which caricatures portray him, but a brainy, active, educated man, conversant with subjects once thought important only in the case of professional men."

Sarah Gates Baird, State Master,
Minnesota Grange, *Address*, 1903

35

The Baird Farmhouse at Edina Mills on West 50th Street just east of Minnehaha Creek, ca. 1910.

Edina Historical Society

Sarah and George Baird of Edina Mills, ca. 1885.

Edina Historical Society

Baird

"*This is Election Day, it is sunny but quite cold. I am baking bread, making yeast and washing...The mail brings George some Holstein pamphlets and me a letter with a Hydrofillum leaf from General LeDuc [Hastings, Minnesota], I am in hopes to grow it...*"

Sarah Gates Baird, *Diary (Vol. 3)*, Edina Mills – March 1886

Prize-winning sheep on the Baird Farm, ca. 1910.

Hennepin History Museum

At the heart of the Edina Mill district, near the crossroads of present-day West 50th Street and Wooddale Avenue, four farms existed that were managed by women and men of exceptional gifts and vision whose efforts took them to fame far beyond their village borders.

The legacy of their individual and collective efforts on behalf of the citizens of the State of Minnesota becomes an even greater astonishment to us when we consider that they lived in immediate proximity to each other. Nothing less than the founding of the Minnesota State Grange, the Minnesota State Agricultural Society, the Minnesota School of Agriculture, the American Society of Agronomy, and the Minnesota State Horticultural Society would

do for these extraordinary eight individuals. As if still not enough, they would promote state prize-winning sheep, national prize-winning horses, international prize-winning cattle, a variety of apples that would become the regional favorite for the next 150 years, and a strong push for women's rights to equal education.

The Bairds

Sarah Gates, a St. Anthony blacksmith's daughter and a schoolteacher, married George W. Baird in 1865 and they settled on his 120-acre farm at Edina Mills just east of Minnehaha Creek. After living in a modest two-story frame farmhouse for nineteen years, the Bairds built a magnificent Victorian brick

The view east from the present-day Sunnyslope neighborhood across the millpond towards the Browndale Farm, ca. 1890.

Edina Historical Society

mansion in 1886 and rebuilt the barn and windmill, a reflection of their prosperity and significant standing in the community.

The Bairds raised purebred Hackney horses and Holstein cattle and are credited with bringing the first sheep into this part of the state, becoming regular State Fair prizewinners for the Merino breed. George Baird, with neighbor Jonathan Taylor Grimes, was co-organizer of the new Minnesota State Agricultural Society.

Having always been active citizens of Edina Mills, the Bairds were also highly invested members of the Minnehaha and Minnesota State Granges. Sarah Baird was editor of the first edition of the Grange newspaper *The Minnehaha Spray* and served eighteen years as State Master of the Grange. George was treasurer of the Minnehaha Grange at the time of his death in 1916. Sarah Baird died in 1923 and, at the time of her death, was thought to have lived longer in Hennepin County than any other living resident. She left a legacy to the State of Minnesota in the form of thirty daily diaries covering every aspect of farm life at Edina Mills from 1882 through 1918. The diaries, a gift from the City of Edina to the state, are held in trust at the Minnesota Historical Society.

At Browndale Farm, ca. 1890.

The Browns

Henry Francis and Sarah Fairchild Brown were prosperous city dwellers in the lumber and flour milling businesses in 1860s Minneapolis. They were noted society figures, giving much of their time and personal fortune to social service and philanthropic organizations and building for themselves the first house in Minneapolis with indoor plumbing (bringing in specially-trained workmen from Chicago for the task).

Henry and Sarah Brown bought land for a stock farm at Edina Mills just northeast of the millpond, and they christened their new farm 'Browndale.' The land, which included the old Edina Mill and millpond, became the site of a magnificent summer house and outbuildings—barns and greenhouses, an electric plant and full water supply—and equally magnificent Scotch-bred Shorthorn and Jersey cattle and Clydesdale horses: the Browndale stock took blue ribbons at every Minnesota State Fair for decades and were the sweepstakes prize winners at the 1893 Chicago World's Fair.

The reputation of Browndale Farm and its stock quickly drew fascinated visitors—and very serious buyers—from around the state, then the country, and finally the world. It was common to have Browndale Shorthorns shipped overseas to Europe and Great Britain.

Browndale Farm's Scotch-bred Shorthorns and Jersey cattle were consistent national prize-winners, ca. 1890.

Edina Historical Society

At home in Hennepin County, the Browndale Farm was setting the fashion for the 'gentleman's farm' and similar holdings were appearing in much of the western area of the county, especially around Lake Minnetonka. Henry's nephew Earle—best known today as the first Hennepin County Sheriff and founder of the Minnesota Highway Patrol—was a frequent visitor to the Browndale Farm and would many years later replicate his uncle's success at his own farm north of Minneapolis at Brooklyn Park.

Sarah Fairchild Brown remained a prominent Minneapolis society hostess and the Browns entertained lavishly at their 'summer home' at Browndale Farm. A brilliant, warm, and gracious woman, Sarah Brown was chosen to be a member of the Women's Board of Managers at the Chicago Worlds Fair, and was later appointed by Governor Knute Nelson to a committee of five members to select a design for the Minnesota state flag.

When Sarah died in 1906 after forty-one years of marriage, Henry withdrew from life at Browndale and returned to the city. After his death in 1912, the last stock auctions were held, drawing more than 400 visitors and overwhelming the auctioneers with bids for virtually every furnishing on the farm. The winning bid for the livestock came sealed from the Montana Ranch Company and the cattle were shipped west by rail. The land, with the

At Browndale Farm, ca. 1890. The farm was among the largest in the district, rivaled only by Col. William S. King's 'Lyndale Farm' one mile east at Lake Harriet.

Edina Historical Society

mill, remained untended until the 1920s when Thorpe Bros. Realtors purchased the Browndale Farm lands and mill for the new Country Club development.

The Bulls

James Alvah and Mary Comstock Bull purchased a farm at Edina Mills in 1857 directly across the Eden Prairie Road (present-day West 50th Street) from George and Sarah Baird. The farm today would be bounded on the north by West 50th Street, France Avenue on the east, and Wooddale Avenue on the west. Minnehaha Creek cut at an angle through the farmlands. For the sum of $3,000 the Bulls received 160 acres, oats and wheat for first plantings, two cows, two brood sows, twelve chickens, a team of oxen, a wagon, farm machinery, a log house and a log barn. The Bulls make their reputation raising dairy cattle and—like the Bairds—sheep, particularly the Shropshire breed.

Mary Comstock died in 1865 and, in 1866, James married Amie Lea Cooper, the daughter of Quaker farmers at Interlachen, a northerly district of Edina Mills. James and Amie became leading members of Edina Mills society. James would be the first Master of Edina's Minnehaha Grange, donating a parcel of the Bull farmland at present-day Wooddale Avenue and West 50th Street to build a new

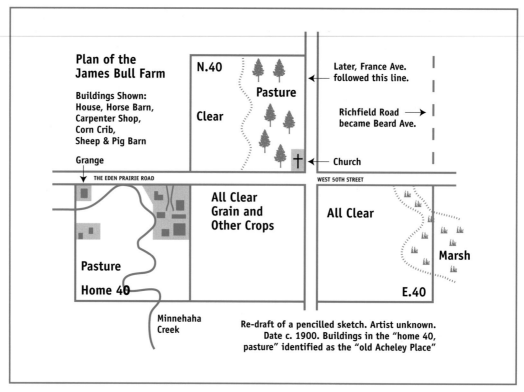

**Plan of the
James Bull Farm**

Buildings Shown:
House, Horse Barn,
Carpenter Shop,
Corn Crib,
Sheep & Pig Barn

Grange

N.40

Clear

Pasture

Later, France Ave.
followed this line.

Richfield Road
became Beard Ave.

Church

THE EDEN PRAIRIE ROAD

WEST 50TH STREET

All Clear
Grain and
Other Crops

All Clear

Pasture

Home 40

Minnehaha
Creek

Marsh

E.40

Re-draft of a pencilled sketch. Artist unknown.
Date c. 1900. Buildings in the "home 40,
pasture" identified as the "old Acheley Place"

Plan of the James Bull Farm, Edina Mills, ca. 1900.

Edina Historical Society

Bull

*"One day [in 1862] Father had gone up to Minneapolis with
produce to get supplies [7 miles by wagon road]. The soldiers
were commandeering every possible conveyance to rush a lot of
soldiers to St. Cloud to quell a reported outbreak by [Sioux]
Indians. Father was told that he could go along and drive if he
wished but his team and wagon were 'in service' right then. He
found George Baird and told him the circumstance, also that his
wife Mary was ill. Baird said he would see that all was cared for
at home…"*

Coates Preston Bull, Letter, Edina, 1962

Reunion of the Bull and Cooper families at the Bull Farm, ca. 1880.

Edina Historical Society

hall. Bull was also a co-founder of the Minnesota School of Agriculture in 1885 and was eventually elected first Master of the Minnesota State Grange in the 1890s.

Amie Cooper Bull was also an active member of Edina's Minnehaha Grange, becoming Chairwoman of the State Grange Women's Committee. She lobbied the Minnesota legislature intensely for the establishment of a program for women, having always believed that farm girls should have equal opportunity for an education. At the time her husband James was organizing the University's Agricultural School in 1885, Amie Bull was appointed by the Minnesota Grange to plead the cause of farm girls in Washington, D.C. Initial courses

of study for women in Home Economics were organized at the University of Minnesota in 1897, largely through the efforts of the Bull family.

Of five Bull children, three achieved considerable reputation of their own in Minnesota education affairs: Mary L. Bull (1863-1928) held a faculty appointment in Home Economics until her death in 1928 and a University scholarship continues to be awarded annually in her name. Alvah Milton Bull (1869-1945) ended his University career as Superintendent of Buildings and Grounds for both city campuses. Coates Preston Bull (1872-1967) was Professor of Agronomy at the University's School of Agriculture, leaving that post in 1919

The Women's Committee of the Minnesota State Grange, 1897-1898. Annie Cooper Bull of Edina Mills is at top center.

Bull

"In September 1866 I gave up teaching and came out here to try housekeeping where I still remain. I also gave up almost all society except for my own people for with my family and the household chores I had not much time for anything else. In 1875 the Grange was organized in this neighborhood, the greatest blessing that ever came to farmers and their families. Many neighbors had lived within a mile from each other and had never met. The Grange meetings called them twice a month to leave their cares behind and to feed their minds. Some of my best friends are now those I found in the Grange…"

Amie Lee Cooper Bull, Letter, Edina Mills ca. 1915

Grazing cattle at Minnehaha Creek, Bull Farm, Edina Mills, ca. 1900.

to work with the Minnesota Department of Agriculture. He was the founder of the American Society of Agronomy and organized their Crop Improvement Association.

James Alvah Bull died at Edina Mills in 1908 and Amie Cooper Bull in 1920, at which time the last forty acres of the old Bull farm were sold for $1,000 an acre.

The Grimes'

Jonathan Taylor and Eliza Gordon Grimes were the first settlers in the Edina Mills district, establishing their sixteen-acre 'Lake Calhoun Nursery' in 1858 with a small house and apple orchards. Jonathan Grimes purchased the Edina mill a year later and improved it with a new dam and spillway. The Grimes family would own the Edina Mill for eight years.

The mill became a critical source of grain for troops at Fort Snelling during the early years of the Civil War, running twenty-four hours a day to meet the requisition demand. So regularly did Jonathan Grimes make the run to Fort Snelling in those years that he claimed his horse could walk the route by memory when lack of sleep took over. Grimes, traveling alone, would wake up to find himself near home after a long nap in the wagon bed.

It was during the early pioneering years that Jonathan Grimes honed his personal philosophy of spiritualism and abolitionist

Eliza Gordon Grimes, ca. 1864.

Edina Historical Society

Jonathan Taylor Grimes, ca. 1874.

Edina Historical Society

Grimes

"*We are all well and pretty well satisfied with our present location. The winter is more severe than we have been used to but the country is very healthy and with this 'luxury' we are content. The other side of the picture with us is this—a good appetite and provisions at the following rates: pork $8.30 per barrel, flour $8.50, cornmeal $1.50 per bushel, dried fruit $.15 per pound, butter $.35, ham $.18, eggs $.75 per dozen, etc. etc...*

Jonathan and Eliza Grimes, Letter, 1856

beliefs, setting himself at once apart from his more conservative neighbors but also endearing himself to the many Quaker families that lived nearby. Fellow pacifists from the district and beyond sought out Grimes at his farm as his reputation grew and a strong network of relationships developed.

Henry David Thoreau visited Grimes at Edina Mills during a journey west in the first year of the Civil War, 1861, drawn by a love of apple trees and an abiding conviction in abolitionist philosophy. Thoreau's journey to Minnesota constituted the only trip he made from New England into the American interior and was the longest trip of his life. He had been in poor health for some months. In the spring of 1861, still ailing, Thoreau finally accepted the medical advice urged on him by well-meaning family and friends and made plans to place himself in the healthier air of Minnesota, a state which was being heavily promoted as a healthy climate (in happy disregard for heat, humidity, mosquitos, and black-flies) and had been a popular destination of tourists for a decade.

Thoreau ordered from the decade-old Minnesota Historical Society its modest but useful publications collection, which he mastered before departure and carried with him for reference.

Henry David Thoreau at New Bedford, Massachusetts shortly after his return from his Minnesota journey in the summer of 1861 and one year before his death. Thoreau had traveled to the American Midwest for his health, anticipating cooler, drier weather. He found the summer climate in Minnesota to be unhappily hot and humid.

49

In a letter of May 3, 1861, Thoreau wrote:

"I have concluded it will be most expedient for me to try the air of Minnesota, say somewhere about St. Paul. I am only waiting to be well enough to start. I hope to get off within a week or ten days. I shall have to study my comfort in travelling to a remarkable degree,—stopping to rest, etc., if need be…"

At the midpoint of his Minnesota journey, Thoreau took lodging near Lake Harriet and was introduced to Jonathan Grimes, a man very much like Thoreau himself: highly educated, abolitionist, spiritualist, and an avocational naturalist. Grimes spoke in his memoirs with delight of Thoreau's visits and of their common links of apples, abolition, and nature.

Thoreau and Grimes were the same age, 43, born in the year 1818, and they became fast friends in mind and heart. Thoreau walked the few miles west from Lake Harriet to the farm on the creek, taking his meals at the family table and wandering the orchards with Grimes, talking of abolition and the war, of the future of the nation, of Truth, of Spirit.

Thoreau left Edina Mills and the Minneapolis lakes in mid-June of 1861, bidding the Grimes family good-by and embarking by steamboat up the Minnesota River to witness what would be the last federal annuity payment to the Dakota tribes assembled at the Lower Sioux Agency at Fort Ridgley.

Long after Thoreau's visit, in the years following the Civil War, Jonathan and Eliza Grimes developed an enormously successful experimental tree nursery. The first gingko trees in Minnesota were grown at the Lake Calhoun Nursery, as were catalpas and many strains of winter-hardy shrubs. Experiments with winter-hardy fruit trees resulted in the development of the Jonathan apple, a great Minnesota favorite, and the Grimes farm became famous. The nursery prospered and, in 1869, the Grimes' built an elegant new farmhouse which became famous for its beauty and its surrounding orchards.

The Lake Calhoun Nursery became a principal greenery source for the City of Minneapolis, supplying the shade trees that still border Hennepin, Lyndale, and University Avenues in Minneapolis. It was Jonathan Grimes' reputation in the region that brought him the honor of serving as the first president of the Minnesota State Horticultural Society.

Eliza died in 1902, Jonathan a year later in 1903. Their children gradually sold parcels of the original farm holding, much of which was platted for Edina's present-day neighborhood of Morningside.

West shore, Lake Harriet, late 1800s. Thoreau stayed for some weeks during June of 1861 at a boarding house in the wooded land between Lake Harriet and Lake Calhoun, and roamed the shores of Lake Harriet in search of botanical specimens which he noted carefully in his journal.

The Past

"*During the '60s I had one unusual experience. Mr. Henry D. Thoreau, poet-naturalist, came to Minnesota on account of his health. He boarded with a Mrs. Hamilton who had an exclusive board-ing house on the shore of Lake Calhoun...As Mr. Thoreau was a lover of trees and flowers he often visited with me and one can imagine the pleasures Mr. Thoreau must have had from roaming through Linden Hills when Lake Harriet was surrounded by a virgin forest...*"

Jonathan Taylor Grimes, *Memoir*, Edina Mills 1898

52

"Veterans of Minnesota Horticulture," 1897. Jonathan Taylor Grimes (at far left in the first row) served as the first presi-dent of the Minnesota State Horticultural Society.

Minnesota Historical Society

*M*any freed Black families…settled after the war in the western half of Richfield Township and, over the ensuing decades, became deeply involved in…the civic, educational, and social affairs of the village…

53

One of Edina's many Black pioneering families, possibly the Yanceys, ca. 1890. Identification research on many of the photographic images of the community's Black families continues to this day.

Edina Historical Society

Will Gillespie, age 14, ca. 1860. The young man made his was north to Minnesota after the Civil War and stayed to farm at Edina Mills.

Edina Historical Society

This school class group includes Madeline (2), Emma (18), and Ellen (21) Gillespie, and Ernestine Siggers (23). (n.d.)

Edina Historical Society

Local legend tells the story of how, in 1865, at the end of the Civil War, a southern white landowner traveled to Minnesota and stopped in Richfield Township, bringing with him six freed slaves and buying for each of them land on which to settle and make a home. It is a compelling and humane story and, as with many such stories of the Civil War years concerning the Underground Railroad and the resettlement of freed Blacks in the North, *anecdotal*, not easily provable by available documentation.

What is certainly true is that many freed Black families, perhaps aided by white Quaker and Episcopalian families, settled after the war in the western half of Richfield Township and,

over the ensuing decades, became deeply involved in community life—very often as leaders—in the civic, educational, and social affairs of the village.

In a span of seventy years, from just after the Civil War through the mid-1930s, at least seventeen Black family names—Byley, Carson, Fyte (Fite), Gillespie, Gleason, Joice, Joy, Leonard, Lucas, Mitchell, Payne, Pittman, Sigger, Staples, Stoddard, Washington, and Yancey—are associated with Edina. The census records reflect varying spellings of first names and we know only a few of the origins of the family names, but there are records indicating that the Washingtons took their name from the Southern plantation family that had

Ellen Maria Bruce Yancey, known as "Nana," ca. 1915.

Edina Historical Society

Beverly Claiborne (B.C.) Yancey, ca. 1900, one of many black pioneers farming near the crossroads of Edina Mills after the Civil War.

Edina Historical Society

Yancey

"Mae Yancey, daughter of an ex-slave, was our Sunday School superintendent. She was a good singer, too. She taught me to play the organ. This was about 1893. There were several [black] families around Edina then, and we were all friends and neighbors together. When Mae got married to a man from Canada and was going to move away, they had a big farewell reception for her at her folks' and the place was packed as she was so well thought of. We were there, of course..."

Ellen (Butterfield) Stubbs, *Minnesota Memories 1887-1917*

owned them as slaves, a common occurrence in the pre-war South; it may be assumed that this was the case with other families that resettled from the southern states.

Their birthplaces, when recorded in the census records, are noted as generally east and south of Minnesota—Ohio, Washington, D.C., Indiana, Kentucky, and North Carolina. George Washington had recently been mustered out at Chattanooga, Tennesse at the rank of Corporal from Company G, 18th U.S. Colored Regiment of St. Paul. There is also a clear connection to Canada where family or friends who had continued north over the border via the Underground Railroad had resettled. Many of the early settlers at Edina

Mills moved on to Canada within five years, and several of the second generation married Canadians and resettled there.

Many of Edina's Black families stayed in the local community for several generations—the Yancey family name is a constant through many decades of Edina census records—while other names appear once and then are gone at the next census taking. Occupations listed over years of census records tell us that many of the families were farmers (the Yanceys were indicated as "fruitgrowers"), day laborers, housekeepers, or servants in other households; the children were at times listed as 'students' or 'scholars'. Plat maps of the village at the turn of the century, and again in the mid-'teens, do

Berry picking on the Yancey fruit farm at Edina Mills, ca. 1890. Beverly and Ellen Yancey are at the far right rear. Edina Mills was a fully integrated and color-blind community well before the turn of the century.

Edina Historical Society

Charles (C.B.) Yancey, ca. 1920. He eventually became Registrar of Deeds for Hennepin County, later retiring in the county's far western district of Independence where many of Edina's second generation of pioneering Black families had settled on farms.

not show any of Edina's Black families in ownership of land and it may be assumed that those who were farming were 'tenant' on their acres.

The pioneering Black families of Edina appear to have moved easily through the public and social life of the village, and memoirs of many of their neighbors point to a true color-blindness, naming Black family members but not describing them in any other way except by profession ("berry farmer" "stabler") or by proximity "from the next farm over"). Ellen Butterfield Stubbs, born in 1883 to white Edina settlers who would eventually work with the Bull family to see the second generation of Black families well settled above Lake Minnetonka, tells us in her memoirs that she played frequently among the children of the Fyte, Staples, and Gillespie families, and describes her delight in attending the wedding of one of the Yancey daughters to a Swedish farmer, Claus Johnson, from an adjacent farm.

It would not be until the years just after the First World War, when Samuel Thorpe developed the elegant Edina Country Club residential district on the old Browndale farm around the mill crossroads with restrictive deed covenants in place, that Edina's Black community would feel estranged.

Thorpe Bros.' building restrictions guaranteed to any buyer, in an era when municipal zoning

Edina School, sixth grade class, 1917.

Edina Historical Society

was nonexistent, that their property would be "safe" from devaluating circumstances, stating that Blacks were explicitly ineligible to buy in the district. Racist deed restrictions were later found unconstitutional by the Supreme Court but, in the 1920s, such restrictions were common and acceptable to enforce segregation: indeed, Thorpe had patterned his restrictions after the Kansas City Country Club District, the model he had employed when designing Edina's new luxury residential development. By the late 1930s virtually all of Edina's Black families had moved into Minneapolis and an historic era had ended for the village.

The Yanceys

Of the sixteen black pioneer families noted, the Yancey family figures most prominently in Edina's history. Ellen and Beverly (B.C.) Yancey operated a successful berry farm on the old Eden Prairie Road (present-day Eden Avenue) just west of the Baird farm. Their establishment in the community was greatly enabled by the Bull family, devout Quakers and longtime sympathizers with the Underground Railroad effort who—with aid from the Butterfields as well—would later assist the second generation of Edina's black pioneers in settling on farms out to the northwest of Lake Minnetonka at Maple Plain and Independence Township.

Many second-generation Black families moved out to the west and north of Edina. This threshing crew, ca. 1910, includes Willie Washington (2nd from left, front row) who married Edina's Phebe (Phoebe) Yancey.

61

Ellen Yancey founded the first PTA for Edina's School District No. 17 in the late 1880s and served as its first president. B.C. Yancey was among the Edina Mills pioneers who met to bring about the incorporation of the Village of Edina in 1888, serving as recorder for the historic debate and vote. He was soon elected as a Justice of the Peace, and in later years re-elected several times as village recorder. At the end of his life, in 1940, he published the *Atlas of the Village of Edina*, now an invaluable aid to the study of local land usage in an era when county plat atlases where far less detailed. Both of the senior Yanceys were early and active members of Edina's Minnehaha Grange No. 398, and the Grange hall itself was moved to the property of a Yancey daughter when the building's original ground lease at West 50th Street and Wooddale Avenue expired in 1934.

The Yancey children followed their parents' examples in community involvement, participating in the Grange's youth activities and attending Edina's School District No. 17. At least one child, Mae, went on to study at the University of Minnesota. Mae Yancey was a popular young woman in the village, playing the organ for the Episcopal congregation that met in the schoolhouse and later at the tiny Trinity Chapel built just down the road,

The Charles Yancey Family, 1917.

Edina Historical Society

supervising its Sunday school. Charles (C.B.) served as both treasurer and clerk to the Edina school board and was appointed to the post of Village Clerk for eight years, from 1912 to 1920: his portrait hangs today in the city's council chambers. He went on to serve as Registrar of Deeds for Hennepin County until his retirement. Like many of Edina's second generation of Black families—grandson Beverly Jr., Phebe, and Maggie Yancey, Willie Washington, and Jeff Fyte—Charles eventually resettled in Hennepin County's Independence Township on the northwest side of Lake Minnetonka.

Beverly Yancey, Sr. died in 1905 at the age of 78, Ellen in 1915 at age 82 and are buried with two of their children—Charles and Helen (Ellen Amelia)—at Minneapolis' Oak Hill Cemetery. The generation of Yanceys, Fytes, and Washingtons who resettled northwest of Lake Minnetonka are buried in Lewis Cemetery in Independence.

Chapter 6

*A*n agricultural village, the only settlement at the crossing of the Minnehaha Creek, where there is a post office, a mill, and a store, and proudly aspires to the dignity of a trading town...The numerous farms are well cultivated, and are occupied by intelligent people who appreciate education, and surround themselves with the accessories of a highly refined society."

R.J. Baldwin, writing about the Village of Edina in Atwater & Stevens' *History of Minneapolis and Hennepin County*, 1895

Edina School picnic at Minnehaha Falls, 1902.

Hennepin History Museum

At the Turn of the Century

A visitor to Edina's millpond, ca, 1900. Though the mill had ceased operations by the turn of the century, the rustic building and graceful millpond had become popular sightseeing destinations for weekend tourists from the city.

The Edina School, built in the late 1880s, stood at the site of the present-day town hall at West 50th Street and Normandale Road. This image was taken shortly after building.

Edina Historical Society

By the first decade of the new century residential development in northern Edina had stabilized, existing mostly as pastoral districts of bungalows and foursquare frame houses set on deep wooded lots, many with extensive gardens and outbuildings. The mill was now outstripped in its importance by the Minnehaha Grange (as the official village hall), the Edina School, and the Craik store and post office. A new creamery had been built to serve the village's north district dairy farmers. Small berry and market garden farms stretched away to the south and the west beyond the mill crossroads.

The inter-urban streetcar line, first laid out in the 1880s and dormant for some years, was in service again by 1905, running west from Minneapolis' Linden Hills district at Lake Harriet into the Edina neighborhoods known as Morningside and Brookside, then out through Hopkins on its way to Lake Minnetonka. The availability of steady service on this commuter streetcar line had greatly influenced the platting and development of Morningside and its neighboring district of Brookside as well as the stretches of France Avenue a half-mile north and south of the village's commercial district at West 50th Street.

Minneapolis families were attracted by the quiet, wooded community and, by streetcar or by carriage along unpaved roads, they came out to Edina to consider establishing a home

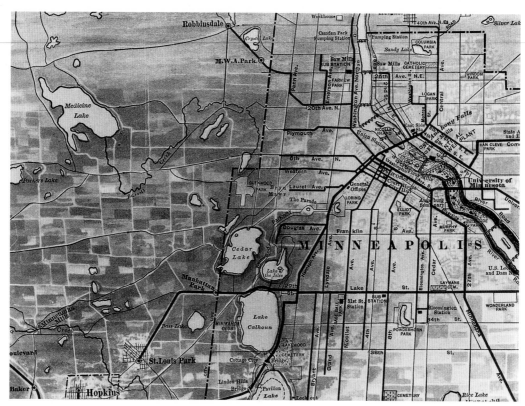

Detail of a map of the Twin Cities Lines, an interurban streetcar service, ca. 1920. Note the Edina stops named for prominent farms or districts: Grimes, Browndale, Brookdale, also the Mendelssohn Station near the Minneapolis Threshing Company over the Hopkins border.

Street Cars

The inter-urban streetcar line, first laid out in the 1880s and dormant for some years, was in service again by 1905, running west from Minneapolis' Linden Hills district at Lake Harriet into the Edina neighborhoods known as Morningside and Brookside, then out through Hopkins on its way to Lake Minnetonka...

Civil War veterans of a Minnesota regiment, ca. 1910. Edina's Preston Cooper stands in the front row, second from the right.

Hennepin History Museum

among the many market gardeners, city professionals, and smallhold farmers that lived in the rolling hills or along the creeksides of the pretty village. The school was thought to be very good, there were several well-established churches, there were four or five small businesses doing well at the village center—a general store, a feedstore, a blacksmith, a post office, and the creamery—and though the Grange was somewhat mysterious to many city dwellers, it was clear that there was a busy social life at the nucleus of the village.

The village offered city folks of relatively modest means the opportunity to have what the monied Minnetonka families had long cherished: a pastoral life, clean air, gardens, quiet, with nearby city services and transportation to jobs and cultural activities intown. Most village lots ran deep and wide, and families planted small orchards and built henhouses and beehives at the backs of their properties after the house had been raised. It was not uncommon to find a cow or goat tethered within a small croft under the trees.

The old foursquare farmhouse style was still a favorite in 1900 but the new fashion of craftsman bungalow—deep verandas, artistic window and woodwork treatments, stucco instead of woodframing—was becoming increasingly popular. Several builders, especially Niels Leerskov, began to make a name for themselves.

In the southern districts, where roads were fewer, Cahill remained a self-sufficient and insular farming community. Here the land remained far more open and the farm holdings much larger, with many farmers still planting grains and harvesting sizeable crops every year for the city markets. St. Patrick's Church, rebuilt in 1884 after a fire, remained the vital spiritual center to life in the Irish Catholic community, and the one-room Cahill School continued as the educational and civic meetinghouse.

The affairs of Cahill life, different as it was from the 1900s suburban market-garden life of the northern district, preoccupied the representatives to village government. Indeed, the needs of the Cahill district were very much as they had been since the Civil War: while the northern districts were considering the questions of telephones and electricity, bridges and road maintenance, Cahill would not see electricity until the 1930s. Cahill representatives to the village government held their own among their more sophisticated neighbors to the north, arguing vigorously for conservative spending on such seeming luxuries as utilities and road repair and fire rigs.

Nevertheless, by the first decade of the new century it became increasingly important to the Cahill community that roads remain open and well maintained as the second generation of Cahill's Irish, like the villagers in the north

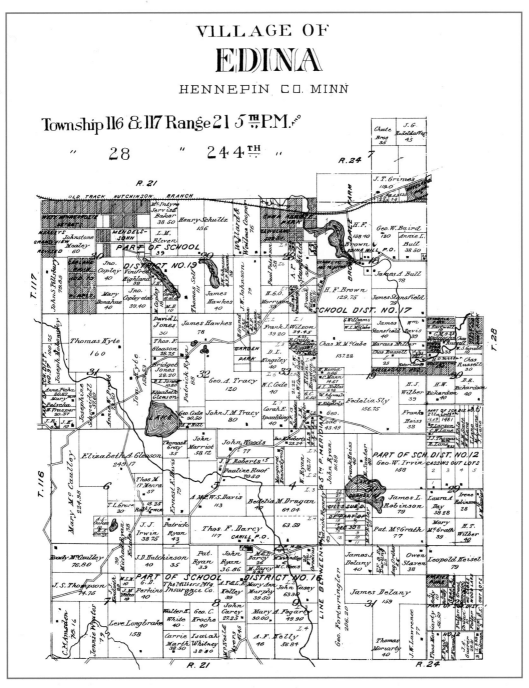

The Village of Edina in 1898. Note the density of small vegetable and berry farms in the northern and eastern districts of the village. Within a few years, the old Grimes farm at the far northeastern corner of Edina would be sold for a new suburban commuter development called 'Morningside.'

A Mdewakanton Dakota family at Shakopee, ca. 1925. Dakota families made their way north from reservations along the Minnesota River up into the southwestern Hennepin County farm villages well into the 1930s to visit among friends on the way to summer encampments on the shores of Lake Minnetonka.

Eden Prairie Historical Society

end, began to move beyond the old boundaries of their farms to seeks services, advanced schooling, and jobs.

Moving Beyond the Borders

Life in rural southwestern Hennepin County required strong ties with one's neighbors and, in the first decades of the new century, the Village of Edina maintained critically interdependent relationships with her neighboring communities of Minneapolis, Richfield (Mills), Bloomington, Eden Prairie, Minnetonka (Township), St. Louis Park, and Hopkins.

The political boundaries that separated Edina from these neighbors were imaginary lines drawn in time and space and had at no time served as barriers to a neighbor's farm, employment up the road, goods and services across a municipal border, second generation homesteads in the next town, shared school districts, or friendships formed in the pioneering days of the Minnesota Territory. The county's territorial roads, based on earlier Native American trails, tied townships and villages together and had been carrying foot and horse and cart traffic for nearly a century.

Now, at the turn of the century, Dakota tribal families traveling north from their Minnesota River reservations passed regularly through Bloomington, Edina, Eden Prairie, and Minnetonka Township en route to Lake

Main Street in Richland (later Richfield) Mills, 1863. Richfield Mills was a near neighbor and important supply source for Edinans in the east and north village districts. The view is south from the millsite at Minnehaha Creek along present-day Lyndale Avenue towards West 53rd Street.

Richfield Historical Society

Minnetonka and the far western border of the county, stopping to visit among long-time acquaintances in the rural districts and renewing old friendships for another season. Many Lake Minnetonka families in the shore communities had regular summer visits from Dakota families and, because many of these same Lake Minnetonka families originated in or married into such Edina pioneering families as the Butterfields, Stubbs, and Yanceys, long-standing friendships with second and often third generation Dakota families remained well-knit well beyond the First World War.

The village of Richfield, formed when the old Richfield Township was split in the 1880s, was just downstream along Minnehaha Creek and there was much traffic between the mills and commercial districts of the two villages. Settled well before Edina, the pioneer families of Richfield Mills, as it was once known, were of critical support to families moving west out of Fort Snelling. General Bartholomew's house at Wood Lake in southeastern Richfield had built in the early 1850s and had long served as important stop-off for travelers to Bloomington, Edina, and Eden Prairie. Now Wood Lake, like Edina Mills, was also developing, growing towards the village center at the north on the creek, and questions of schools and services were debated among the Richfield and Edina families when they met to trade or visit.

LINDEN HILL DAIRY
VIC BAKKE
EDINA

Bloomington Township on the southern border of Edina was a district of great beauty, sited on the Minnesota River along its southern border and graced with abundant wooded hills, rich farmland, beautiful lakes, and a swift-flowing creek named 'Nine Mile' for its exact distance to the Fort Snelling Reserve. Bloomington's Oak Grove district above the Minnesota River was, like Richfield Mills and Wood Lake, settled much earlier than Edina and thus was an important supply stop for travelers moving west. Once known principally as the site of the Pond Brothers' mission to the Dakota Nation, the district had developed into a true commercial center amidst modest farms. Children living in northwest Bloomington's Bush Lake District attended the Cahill School up the road in Edina when such reciprocity would be have been common for communities sharing school districts.

Bloomington's Bernard Stewart would regularly bring his threshing crew and machinery around to the neighboring districts of Edina, Richfield, Eden Prairie and Hopkins on a per-hire basis, very common at a time when owning costly threshing machinery would have been beyond the means of most small farmer in southwestern Hennepin County. Cooperation among the farmers was the very lifeblood of a successful passage through a year of planting, growing, harvesting, and wintering.

In Eden Prairie, also sited on the Minnesota River, traffic continued to pass northeast through the village into Edina on the way to the Minneapolis markets. The Rowland Store with its adjacent blacksmith shop and post office was a popular source of goods, services and visiting opportunities for farming families living over the border in neighboring southwest Edina. Prior to the building of the Rowland Store, folks living in northeast Eden Prairie would have to travel east to Edina Mills to pick up and drop off mail, frequently taking along a bag of wheat or corn to be ground at the same time. George Bren's berry box company stood on present-day Bren Road south of Shady Oak Lake at the Eden Prairie-Hopkins border and was a popular source of market packaging for many southwest Edina berry and truck farmers.

The Monitor Drill Company in St. Louis Park, a suburb just over Edina's western border along important rail lines out of Minneapolis, provided employment for many Edinans and, as the suburb grew, small factories and light industry became the village's hallmark, providing continuously expanding employment opportunities for many neighboring communities.

Further north along the major rail lines was Hopkins, the largest and most prosperous of the southwest Hennepin County villages and a critical source of goods, services, education

Main street in the Village of Bloomington, ca. 1900. Like many of Edina's neighbors, Bloomington was an important source of supplies and news for southeastern Edina's isolated farming families, and the roads between the two villages were well traveled.

Bloomington Historical Society

Workers at Hopkins' McDonald Feed Mill, ca. 1915. The feed mill, located on present-day Excelsior Boulevard, employed many laborers who traveled in from neighboring communities. Edina's Ben McCauley is at the far left.

Hopkins Historical Society

and employment for a great many Edina families, often traveling regularly up from as far away as the Cahill district. As with Bloomington, Edina shared a school district with Hopkins and many young people from Edina traveled up old Washington Avenue (present-day Highway 169) to the Burnes School. The Campbell Store, one of the largest in the district, stood near the border with Edina and was an important source of supply.

The Minneapolis Threshing Company (later Minneapolis Moline) was the largest manufacturing company west of Minneapolis and a critical employer for men and women from all adjacent communities, many from Edina, for nearly half a century.

The vast campus of the Hennepin County Poor Farm on old Washington Avenue was both employer and, on sad occasion, home to unfortunate folk from nearby towns and villages.

The Hennepin County Fair, a hugely popular annual event staged in central Hopkins, drew attendance from virtually every village and township in the county at a time when the heavy percentage of the population was engaged in farming—truck, berry, or backyard. The fair was a three-day opportunity to show off produce and livestock, catch up on the latest farming concepts, look over the newest machinery, compete in the popular horse races, and see family and friends who had come in from the far corners of the county.

Minneapolis, of course, served as a vital source of employment for Edina's professional and skilled-labor citizens and as the principle marketing venue for Edina's farming community. Most of the city's principal rail lines passed to the north of the market enabling quick shipment of district goods to outstate and out-of-state markets. Most of the county's market gardeners saw their produce sold to local restaurateurs who would pass through the stalls daily and, by 6:00 a.m., would have selected the day's vegetables and meats for the city hotels, upscale restaurants, and corner cafes. A daily ride into town to sell at the city market was the lot of a great many of Edina's farm families, and young children were in frequent attendance to assist with the necessary chores of set-up and selling. Not until the 1940s did Minneapolis city market lessen in importance to Edina farmers as the market gardens gave way to suburban residential development.

In Minneapolis' southwest corner, Lake Harriet a mile to the east of Edina was a popular recreational resource for those living in the eastern and northeastern districts of the Edina, offering picnic grounds, carriage rides, horse races, skating rinks, sleigh rides, hiking clubs, bicycling clubs, and concerts at the bandshell.

Linden Hills, at the end of West 44th Street on Lake Harriet's west shore, was the nearest

Bernard Stewart's threshing rig and team from Bloomington Township, at Hopkins, ca. 1910. Stewart worked on a per-hire basis in the neighboring districts of Richfield, Edina, Eden Prairie and Hopkins at a time when owning costly threshing machinery would have been beyond the means of most smallholding farm families in southwestern Hennepin County.

Hopkins Historical Society

The Minneapolis Threshing Machine Company, Hopkins, ca. 1900. The MTM, later known as Minneapolis Moline, was a principal employer for southwestern Hennepin County.

Minneapolis commercial district to northern Edina and boasted a broad array of goods and professional services. It was a popular shopping resource for north Edina villagers who could board the streetcar anywhere along its route on West 44th Street between Brookside and Morningside. By the end of the first decade of the new century a telephone exchange and lending library were available in Linden Hills, as were a hay and feed store, cleaners, sweet shop, general store, bakery, and moving picture theater. By 1920 Linden Hills had become Edina's primary resource for goods and services, boasting a shoe repair shop, jeweler, five grocers, meat market and delicatessen, gas station and garage, two pharmacies, a dress shop

and milliner, a bicycle shop, a laundry, and numerous professional offices, all heavily patronized by Edina residents.

Before the Great War

By the late 'teens much of Edina's northerly districts had been platted for development and the village's commercial district one-half mile to the east of the old mill crossroads at France Avenue and West 50th Street was steadily growing, undeterred by roads that would not be paved for another decade.

A gradual shift from grain and livestock farms to smaller higher value per-acre truck and dairy farms occurred in the second decade of the century, and these farms often did as

well as their larger neighbors. The number of farms, however, began to drop steadily as urbanization approached from the north, falling from 166 farms in 1895 to 141 farms in 1905, and then to seventy-five farms in 1925.

More significantly, by 1905 half the president population of the village was comprised of people who had lived there less than five years and the new residents represented ethnicities not often seen before in the district, Swedes and Danes and Norwegians. Consequently, in the years before and just after World War I, a number of new Protestant churches were founded in the north end of the village.

Education remained a strong priority for the village and the two-story brick Edina School was expanded several times to accommodate an increasing student population. No argument about the need for such a facility was voiced by a community which had long been committed to the best possible education for its children. But there was a steadily escalating debate between the residents of north Edina and the farming residents of south Edina over issues of street improvement, utilities upgrades, and other such common concerns of suburban communities.

By 1920 the debate was causing a serious rift among the voting citizenry of Edina. More and more frequently the acrimonious debates

The Hennepin County Fair, Hopkins, ca. 1910. The popular annual event was a prime opportunity for regional farm families to display the year's best crop yields and livestock and to socialize with friends and family. The fairgrounds were located at present-day Excelsior Avenue and 11th Avenue, approximately where the Hopkins Theatre now stands.

Hopkins Historical Society

Dawn at the Minneapolis Farmers' Market, ca. 1920. The Market was the principal venue for the county's farm production sales by lot purchase and auction. Most of the farm families in Edina, as in neighboring villages, made their way into town to the city market several times per week.

Edina Historical Society

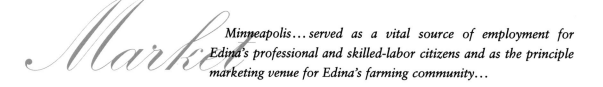

Market

Minneapolis...served as a vital source of employment for Edina's professional and skilled-labor citizens and as the principle marketing venue for Edina's farming community...

were recounted in detail in the local newspapers and, as the pressures of urban life became more evident along the Minneapolis boundary with Edina, such debates began making their way into the bigger city's daily newspapers.

Edina's debates over how best to spend the citizens' dollars took on a sudden significance with the advent of two astonishing and unexpected events that took place almost concurrently in the early 1920s: the proposal by Thorpe Bros.' Realtors to build a new luxury residential district on the old Browndale Farm property at the mill crossroads, and the secession of the entire Morningside district from the northeast corner of the village.

The former would forever alter the economic and social profile of the village, and the latter would forever discomfort the complacent in Edina's civic life.

Employees of the Minneapolis Threshing Machine Company posing for the camera, ca. 1900. The Hopkins manufacturing firm at Excelsior Boulevard at Washington Avenue (present-day Highway 169) was the largest employer in southwestern Hennepin County and prompted the development of several adjacent workers' housing districts such as West Minneapolis Heights and Edina's Mendelssohn district.

Hopkins Historical Society

Now, at the turn of the century, Dakota tribal families traveling north from their Minnesota River reservations passed regularly through Bloomington, Edina, Eden Prairie, and Minnetonka Township en route to Lake Minnetonka and the far western border of the county, stopping to visit among long-time acquaintances in the rural districts and renewing old friendships for another season...

Visiting tribal families encamped on the grounds of the Minnesota State Fair, St. Paul, 1909. The Mdewakanton Dakota community maintained strong relationships with individual farm families through southwestern Hennepin County for a century after federal restriction to reservation life.

Hennepin History Museum

A t the time [1912], France Avenue was not cut through as it is today, there being just a wagon track...there was no car loop or any stores, [we] had to trade at Upton Avenue [in Linden Hills]...we had rural mail delivery service, there were about thirty-five boxes on the corner at France Avenue at 44th Street. Electricity was just being brought into the village. Residents either pumped water by hand or [used] gasoline engines. About three people had windmills—no sewer or gas mains. Several people had [outhouses] in the back yard. Several people kept chickens and some had their own cows, bees... and farmed an acre. The old steam motor line to Excelsior ran about a block south of the streetcar tracks and I can remember very well the old rails and ties. The streetcars were going strong, the line going through to Excelsior. The right of way was all lit up at night with carbon arc lamps..."

Robert S. Jackson who built the family home in
Morningside at 4216 West 44th Street in 1912

83

Constable George Weber at France Avenue and West 44th Street in Morningside's Westgate commercial district.

Minnesota Historical Society

85

This house at 4300 France was built by the Reynolds family in 1905. It was the first house to be built on France Avenue in what became Edina's Morningside district. The northern reaches of Edina surrounding the old mill crossroads became the village's major residential development area.

Edina Historical Society

The Village of Morningside

Morningside has, in its short life, been a neighborhood, a village, and a neighborhood again. Many would say Morningside is also a state of mind, a place apart, beloved and jealously shepherded in the midst of urban giants.

It's a tiny bit of a place, a half-mile square perched on the far northeast corner of Edina and the only segment of Edina that was never part of the old Richfield Township. The district began its life in 1905 as a commuter's pastoral paradise of 3-1/2 acre lots carved out of Jonathan Grimes' orchards and built out along the early streetcar line when the 'nickel limit' on the streetcar line was pushed west through Edina and neighboring Hopkins.

Morningside, like its neighboring districts of Brookside and Browndale Park, was promoted as 'country in the city' and indeed it was that. Many early residents raised substantial gardens, kept bees, tended a cow on their land. The lots were deep and wide, the tree-shaded streets inviting, and the streetcar offered three stops throughout. Paired with reliable and inexpensive transportation and low taxes, electric lights and telephone service, the combination proved irresistible to white-collar workers and professionals and the Morningside neighborhood developed quickly. By 1920 the district could boast almost one-third of a total Edina population of 1,800 and the 'Westgate' shopping district at West 44th

Summer visitors wade in Minnehaha Creek below the mill pond near the Bull Farm, ca. 1900. The pastoral loveliness of the village beyond the Minneapolis city limits had been an attraction for day-trip visitors long before the developers began promoting the healthful lifestyle of country living for urban commuters.

Edina Historical Society

The Reverend Huid Nelson, his wife Viola, his father Peter, and his children on the steps of their newly completed house on Branson Street in Edina's Morningside district, ca. 1915.

Morningside

"It is time Morningside emerged from its chrysalis stage and became a recognized entity instead of being a revenue appendix of 8,500 acres of pasture, woodland, and cornfield. Is there any reason why an intelligent, wide-awake and up-to-date community should not administer its own affairs instead of being governed by "absentee treatment"? We have young men in Morningside—attorneys, bankers, realtors, engineers, contractors and other business and professional men, who are admirably equipped to administer its affairs, whom we would meet face to face daily and who would listen to our requests for service in a sympathetic and respectful attitude..."

Editorial, *Harriet News*, September 13, 1920

Morningside, ca. 1915. Extensive backyard gardens were a promoted feature in the development of Morningside. Many residents also tethered a cow, raised chickens or ducks, or kept bees in the deep lots behind their new homes.

Edina Historical Society

Street and France—which included the handsome Westgate Theatre, the art deco Convention Grill, and the two-story brick Odd Fellows Hall which served as the unofficial 'town hall' of Morningside—was already much larger than the tiny commercial center down the road at West 50th Street

It wasn't a grand residential district like the Country Club community, rather it was handsome, comfortable, the ideal place for middle-class city professionals to raise a family. Teachers, attorneys, accountants, insurance managers, bank managers, engineers, social workers and office executives settled in the Morningside neighborhood of Edina, bringing with them a high level of education and a more sophisticated lifestyle than their neighbors down the road working the market gardens. Many fine houses were built in the years before the First World War, the craftsman bungalow being one style especially well represented on Morningside's streets. The range of bungalow designs—California, Mission, Arts and Crafts—showed the artistic flair of the builders, many serving as both designers and contractors of their own houses. Such consistency of design in the residential housing stock quickly gave Morningside a unique cohesiveness: even today, the first-time visitor can easily define the boundaries of Morningside by examining the residential architecture.

Niels Leerskov built many of Morningside's beautiful bungalows, including this house at 4425 Grimes Avenue. The architect's own home, a handsome Midwest Foursquare frame residence known as the Leerskov House, still stands at 4410 Curve Avenue.

Minnesota Historical Society

Inevitably, with the charm of the setting came the expectation of amenities—streetlights, sidewalks, improved roadways—all considered extravagant by the village councillors who represented the larger rural districts of Edina. Assuredly, in 1911 some requests were deemed reasonable: a deputy constable position was permanently funded. But through the ensuing decade the Morningside Improvement Association locked horns repeatedly with the village council over improvement issues. Only in 1912 did Morningside succeed in having its first neighborhood representative, Niels Leerskov, a popular builder, elected to the village council; though every year after that Morningside had at least one representative

speaking for the district, Morningsiders won few improvement victories for their district of Edina.

By 1920 it was evident that Morningside would continue to grow. A new dry goods store opened in the already-busy Westgate intersection, and a new pharmacy opened in the same year down West 44th Street at Beard Avenue just over the border in Minneapolis, a few blocks out of Morningside. The Odd Fellows Hall was now much more than a lodge and civic meeting hall, it also was housing dance classes, community parties, theater presentations, club meetings, and worship services for the Morningside Congregational community which had outgrown its small

chapel on Morningside Road.

When it was made clear to Morningsiders by the village council that few improvements would funded from city money but would instead need to be born by the individual homeowners, Morningside residents gathered at the Odd Fellows Hall in the autumn of 1920 to discuss secession from the Village of Edina. There was opposition, certainly, including a petition to halt the process on the grounds that Edina was legally too small to permit division into two villages; however, it was proven that Edina was actually among the largest square-mile villages in the county and that were no legal grounds for such a petition.

The final election was held in November 1920 and was notable for having the participation of the first female voter and the first female election judge in Hennepin County history. The vote was close but carried for separation and, after a fiercely angry all-village debate at the Grange Hall, Morningside officially seceded to become a village in its own right. A second, quieter meeting was held in January 1921 to discuss the division of holdings and responsibilities between the old village and the new, and to embark on a new civic history which would endure for forty-six years.

The Country Club District

Though Edina's village council devoutly hoped that the secession of Morningside

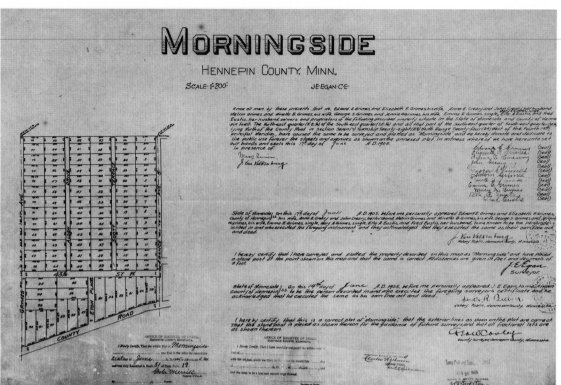

would relieve the village of the burden of unreasonable developmental costs, the community continued to see steady suburban residential building into the 1920s during which Edina's population doubled. Correspondingly, the demands of infrastructural maintenance, utilities, and city services continued to accelerate.

Edina's residential building boom shifted to an altogether higher level when Samuel Thorpe and Thorpe Bros. Realtors purchased the old Browndale and Baird farms in 1922, some 300 acres essentially comprising the entirety of the historic mill district, and proposed to the Village of Edina the creation of an exclusive residential district with every amenity possible, including full membership privileges on an 18-hole golf course. To the delight of the village council, Thorpe intended to underwrite the full cost of developing municipal services to the new district—to a total cost of $1,000 per lot and, on this understanding, the council approved the plan.

Edina's Country Club District, modeled on J.C. Nichols' hugely successful Kansas City Country Club District, was divided into two Sections, Brown and Fairway. The plan called for controlled development, avoiding the standard haphazard development of selling lots from a pattern built on a street grid and then leaving the new owners to build or not, landscape or till, sell or keep, in whatever fashion they wished. Thorpe's plan was entirely different:

The lunch counter at the Convention Grill on Sunnyside Road, ca. 1941. The Convention was a popular restaurant drawing patrons from Edina's northern residential districts and the lakes area neighborhoods of Minneapolis to Morningside's Westgate commercial district.

he designed the District with contoured streets and parks heavy with shade trees, set firm building valuations and design restrictions, and installed all major utility services—water, sewer, gas, and underground electricity—for the 550 platted lots before they were placed on the market in 1924. The golf course with its $60,000 clubhouse was slated to open in June of that same year. Streets and sidewalks were in place before prior to initial site sales, and trees were planted throughout.

The popular Minneapolis architectural firm of Liebenberg & Kaplan was commissioned to design model homes on Edina Boulevard and on Moorland Avenue to promote the new and elegant architectural consistency that would become the hallmark of the district. The designs were much admired by qualified buyers and critically reviewed and discussed in a sequence of Minneapolis newspaper articles accompanying the full-page advertisement Thorpe placed in the Minneapolis newspapers in June of 1924. The first home offered in the district was marketed at a breathtaking $24,000; though building in the Country Club District was initially slowly paced—by 1930, only 270 of the 550 available lots had seen construction—a total of 554 structures were eventually built in the district representing a great range of historic revival designs including American Colonial, English Cottage, Mediterranean, New England Colonial, and

A Woman's Club gathering, Morningside, ca. 1930. The tiny residential district boasted an astonishing range of social, educational, and civic organizations in its forty-six years of existence.

Edina Historical Society

Norman. The 1930 Country Club Directory lists some 250 families living in the exclusive community, a great majority having moved from southwest Minneapolis, and representing 1,032 of the 3,138 residents of the village, one-third of Edina's population.

By 1926 over $1.3 million had been invested in the Country Club District residential buildings and $1 million in amenities and utilities. The first golf clubhouse burned in 1929 but, being deemed indispensable to the life of the community, was immediately replaced with a larger, equally handsome structure.

"Restricted"

Samuel Thorpe wanted the Edina Country Club district to be truly exclusive, a cohesive community. The golf course and club were intended to support this concept but the real signal of exclusivity was the restrictive covenant deed that all owners in the district were required to abide by. Under the provisions of this deed, all buildings and landscape plans in Thorpe Bros.' Country Club District were subject to supervision by a home builders committee, later by a committee of the Country Club Association. All details in design—specifications, elevations, location, grade, and color scheme were subject to review and approval. Out-buildings, fuel storage tanks, and garbage receptacles were to be well hidden, no signage of any kind could be employed, and certain "shedding" trees and shrubs such as poplars

The Danens family cutting hay on empty lots in the Country Club District, 1932.

Edina Historical Society

and box-elders were forbidden.

And more than just trees and paint colors were forbidden: certain classes of people were overtly—and covertly—forbidden to build or live in the Edina Country Club District, and District residents were guaranteed "freedom" from such undesirables by the covenant they signed when purchasing their new home, guaranteeing to buyers, in an era when municipal zoning was nonexistent, that their property would be "safe" from devaluating circumstances. Racist deed restrictions were soon to be found unconstitutional by the Supreme Court but, in the 1920s, such restrictions were acceptable to enforce segregation, and the District's covenant expressly stated that "no lot shall ever be sold, conveyed, leased or rented to any person other than of the white or Caucasian race... except such as may be serving as domestics for the owner or tenant of said lot while owner or tenant is residing thereon." Blacks were, therefore, explicitly precluded from ownership of property in the District, and Jews were implicitly unwelcome. In their time, even the partners of the eminent architectural firm of Liebenberg & Kaplan, builders of the first residential models in the District, would themselves have been ineligible to live there.

Covenant restrictions were as common and accepted in their time as they would be uncommon and unacceptable in our own.

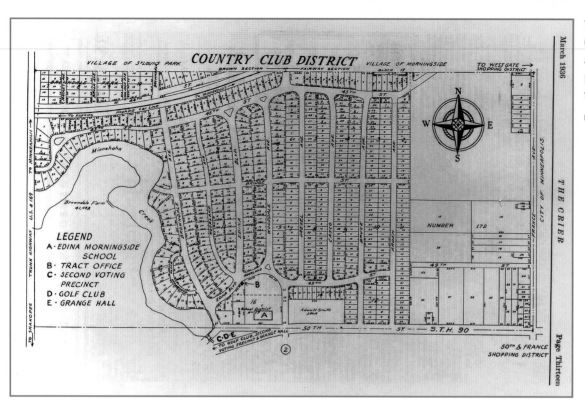

The Edina Country
Club District, from
a mid-development
promotional adver-
tisement, 1936.

Edina Historical Society

95

Nevertheless, the establishment of the Edina Country Club District, and the arrival of 1,000 wealthy, white, and culturally sophisticated adults accustomed to positions of leadership in society lead directly to the departure of Edina's Black community out of civic affairs and elected offices, out of community leadership positions, and finally—inevitably—out of the village altogether by the end of the Second World War.

Anti-semitism, virtually unheard-of in Edina before the First World War, became a haunting hallmark of Edina life. As late as the end of the 1950s, potential buyers known to be Jewish were often openly turned away by realtors and requested to look for residential property elsewhere. It was a gentle compensation that Morningside opened its doors to any who wished to buy there and, through and beyond the war years, saw a prosperous professional Jewish family community settle within its borders.

Accelerated Change

The effects of Samuel Thorpe's Country Club District reached far beyond its exclusive boundaries, forever changing the demographics of the village in which it was built. The commercial district at the crossroads at West 50th Street and France Avenue, unpaved until the late 1920s, grew dramatically as service and retail vendors appeared to support the growing and well-to-do suburban population.

Samuel Thorpe's Country
Club, built 1925.

Edina Historical Society

The pace of automobile traffic through the entire area also greatly accelerated: never a "streetcar suburb," ownership of a Country Club District residence assumed ownership of an automobile (and a late model one at that).

Edina's village council saw the future of suburban development in the advent of the Country Club District: in 1929, after a decade of breakneck residential development which inevitably followed the great success of the Country Club District, Edina became the first village in Minnesota to set in place a comprehensive zoning ordinance, creating a thoughtful, fully articulated planning model and setting the standard for other communities around the state.

Most importantly, Samuel Thorpe's Country Club District would prove to be the critical factor, the one significant event, the reason that Edina is known today as a suburb of exclusivity and wealth: Thorpe's Country Club District spelled the beginning of the end for Edina as a community of quiet market gardeners happy with their streetcars, their Grange hall, their corner telephone box, their unpaved roads.

Here was the future, here were the new suburbanites, wanting admittance to Edina's rolling hills of forested land and farms, wanting a better place to raise the children, a better life, near the city but not in it, with all the amenities of city life and all the luxuries money could buy.

SAMUEL S. THORPE

WHO has for thirty-five years been active in building up both the residence and commercial districts of Minneapolis, has now achieved his greatest desire by developing for Minneapolis a high class restricted suburban district; and to this end has had many conferences with his intimate friend, Mr. J. C. Nichols of Kansas City, who developed the famous Country Club District of that City, and who is recognized as the premier developer of high class residence sections in the United States.

Mr. Nichols and his associates have made many helpful suggestions for the Minneapolis Country Club District and have given Mr. Thorpe the benefit of their years of experience in the matter of arrangement for a high class sub-division, size and shape of building sites, improvements—and particularly restrictions—to make the district beautiful, distinctive and economical.

It is freely predicted that this Minneapolis Country Club District will become as well known as Mr. Nichols' Country Club District of Kansas City, or the famous Shaker Heights development in Cleveland, or Roland Park in Baltimore.

ALONG THE CREEK

CREEKS and lakes are nature's choicest gifts to the artistry of her landscapes. Minnesota is generously endowed with these sparkling adornments. Circumstances, however, do not always permit the rarest beauty spots to become the nucleus for a metropolitan home district. The Country Club District is most fortunate in this respect. Minnehaha Creek, within the boundaries of the Country Club District is really a lake or series of lakes. Lake Minnetonka, which is the source of Minnehaha Creek, furnishes the supply of fresh water; the dam at Fiftieth Street fixes the level of the lake, which is within the confines of the Country Club District.

Thorpe Bros. Realtors' original Edina Country Club District promotional brochure, 1926.

Edina Historical Society

97

"...for the purpose of maintaining a high class, restricted, residential district, free from objectionable or value-destroying features in the Section of the Country Club District in which the premises are located to the end that each lot owner in such Section shall be protected against improvements of an inferior style, character or appearance, which will interfere with the beauty and harmony of a high class restricted residential district, or tend to reduce the value thereof... "

Item 7, Convenant, *Country Club District Indenture Contract, 1926*

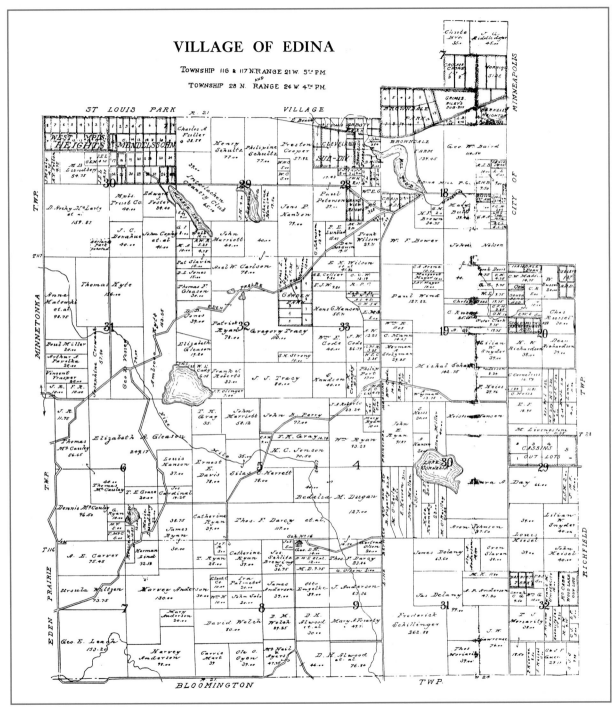

Plat of the Village of Edina, 1913.

eople living in Edina during the first one-third of the twentieth century shared in the tremendous economic and social change which shook the entire nation during that time. Those thirty years saw the prosperity, optimism, and reform of the Progressive era, the trauma of World War I, the disillusioned and business-oriented 1920s, the stock market collapse of 1929, and the beginnings of the Depression and New Deal. Those years saw the creation of a nationwide consumer-oriented economy, a revolution in dress and morals, the rise of radio and motion pictures, and the emergence of the automobile. All of these affected the people of Edina as they affected the rest of the nation..."

Paul D. Hesterman, *From Settlement to Suburb:
The History of Edina, Minnesota* (1988)

99

An Edina Village Council meeting, ca. 1940. Council meetings were held at the Grange hall from 1888 until 1942.

Edina Historical Society

Edina's one-room Cahill School at its original site on West 70th Street and Cahill Road just west of present-day Highway 100, ca. 1935.

Edina Historical Society

Edina and Morningside, as with all the nation, experienced great change in the decades bracketed by the two world wars.

Change came in the form of economic depression, renewed residential development and improved infrastructure, pressure on educational institutions, the founding or expansion of worship communities, and a further widening of the gap between the south and north districts of the village. North Edina, ever-more cosmopolitan in its character and expectations, little resembled Edina's still-rural south districts such as Cahill. On the north end of the village stood substantial housing districts, handsome schools, estates and country clubs. On the south end were the family farms and the rural churches and an aging but much beloved one-room schoolhouse. Only a handful of roads yet connected the north and south ends of the village.

As everywhere in the country, development came to a virtual standstill in Edina during the Great Depression, then soared again in the mid-1930s until the opening of World War II. Population figures rose and fell accordingly, eventually climbing from a 1930 figure of 3,138 to 9,744 in 1950. Budgets for Edina schools were also dependent on the times but as the population steadily increased, the request for the raising and release of more

Edina's Boy Scout Troop No. 44, March 1939.

Memories

"Fiftieth Street was a dirt road when I used to walk to school and I remember when they paved it with cement. Our front yard had several huge oak trees across the front and they had to cut them down to widen the street for paving. Beyond our village at 50th and France, west and south, was a huge field and farm and we used to roam all the way over to the Minnehaha Creek...about 1935 or '36..."

Kenneth Krake, from childhood reminiscences of
growing up at 3917 West 50th Street (at Halifax) in Edina

Hartzell's Edina Garage tow-truck, 1920. The Hartzell Garage expanded from a small repair shop and gas station into a full-fledged Chrysler dealership over forty years of business in Edina's commercial district at West 50th Street and France.

Edina Historical Society

school program funds became a central issue in the village as well as for Morningside residents, still part of School District 17.

By the late 1930s roadways were being improved at a steady pace, though the upgrades were being applied primarily in the northern neighborhoods. Much of downtown Edina remained unpaved beyond the half-mile square district of the commercial center and fire rigs still had to be brought in over muddy roads from Minneapolis' Linden Hills district to serve the northern half of Edina. At times snow and rain dug such deep gouges out of France Avenue's unpaved stretches that the depressions were called 'foxholes' and were a popular source of entertainment for neigh-borhood children. A variety of paving materials were eventually applied to deal with the problem. West 50th Street was paved with concrete, France Avenue with tar for the ten blocks between Morningside's Westgate commercial district at West 44th Street and the far end of Edina's downtown district at West 54th Street. In the 1930s West 50th Street was considered by far the more critical thoroughfare—the two-way stop signs halted traffic on France Avenue to permit through traffic on West 50th Street—thus the more costly and durable paving material. Local residents were hired to plow the paved sections with horse-drawn wooden scrapers.

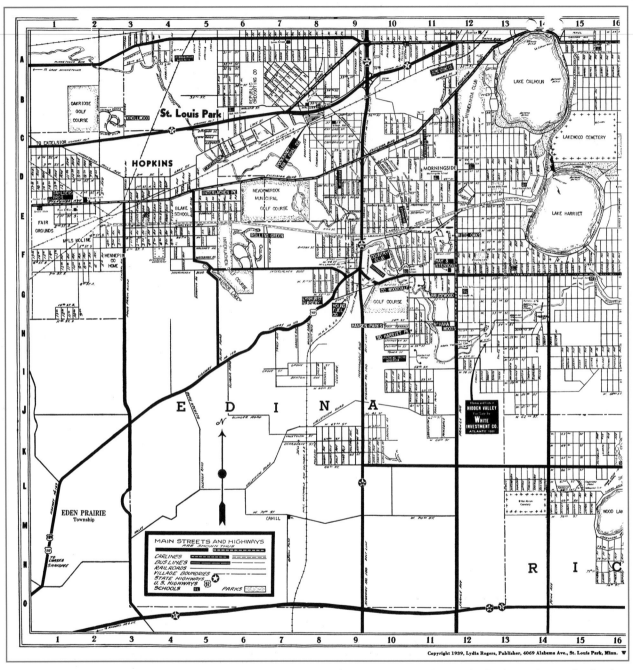

The Village of Edina, 1935. In the decade following the end of World War I, virtually all of Edina's northeasterly districts saw heavy development, leaving the south and west farming districts untouched. Note the presaging of the 1960s freeway expansion in the state highways edging the south and west boundaries of the village.

Edina Historical Society

Many new Protestant congregations were founded in the village in these years and established congregations grew so fast that several new church buildings went into construction to serve the increase in parishioners. St. Stephen the Martyr Episcopal Church was built across from the Country Club District on the old Grange hall site, and the Edina Baptist Church was established at the far end of the downtown district along France Avenue at West 54th Street. Two new Lutheran congregations were established, Calvary Lutheran at Cahill—only the second church to be built in that historic district since the Civil War—and St. Peter's Lutheran up the block from the Edina Baptist community. Morningside's Congregational community soon required a much larger building and, after raising a handsome stone church on Grimes Avenue on the west side of the village, sold its tiny chapel on Morningside Road for use as a residence.

Conflict and Change

The Cahill district of Edina was still a predominantly Irish and Catholic community in the 1930s, centered closely around the crossroads of Cahill Road and West 70th Street, anchored by the Cahill School, St. Patrick's church, and the Cameron's general store. Cahill families wanting a high school education for their children had to transport them to

Edina School's Eighth Grade Class, 1924. Rose Payne's (front row, far right) family was among the last of Edina's Black farming families living in the village after the First World War.

Edina Historical Society

St. Louis Park High School in an old seven-passenger Packard limousine that served as the district's school bus. There were scattered farmsteads and a few homes just nearby the intersection itself. Electricity came in as late is the mid-'30s and few homes had telephones: the Cameron store had a pay-phone which was sufficient for most resident needs. Cahill was, in essence, a rural crossroads community contained within a larger suburban district.

By great contrast, north Edina was bustling and home to an ever-increasingly well-to-do community. The presence of the Country Club District had spurred adjacent residential developments, handsome and well designed,

throughout the village and the new home owners were professionals and administrators, educators and business owners, driving automobiles for the daily ride to the city or taking advantage of the urban commuter streetcar line that provided steady service between Edina and Minneapolis.

The commercial center at West 50th Street and France Avenue, having caught up to the sophistication of Morningside's Westgate district a half-mile north up France Avenue, now offered most of the usual services, including a multitude of grocers (Knutson & Turner, Hove's, Olson & Adolphson, Piggly Wiggly), several dry goods shops (Brauer's 5&10 and

Nelson's), two pharmacies (Gregg's and Nelson's), plenty of cafes, bakeries, and beer parlors (Creiman's, Nolans, Brown Derby, Hoyt's, Sonny's Hamburgers, Hasty Tasty), two ice cream and sweet shops (Forberg's and the Edina), the Town & Country Floral Shop (later Bachman's in 1939), Anthonie's Frock Shop, Barry's Hardware and Sporting Goods, Hartzell's Chrysler-Plymouth automobile dealership and garage, Hay & Stenson's Liquor Store, Bert's Barbershop, Erickson's Beauty Shop, and Michael Davitt's new Edina Realty offices.

The new Edina Theatre was built in 1934 on the site of the old Elgin Creamery barns. A fanciful art deco creation by the Liebenberg & Kaplan (of Country Club District architectural fame), the theater was designed with flanking cafes and air-conditioned by cool water from an artesian well. The first movie to show at the new theater was Shirley Temple's *On the Good Ship Lollipop:* multitudes attended the gala public opening. A new medical office was built a block out of the district, another eye-catching art deco design in white concrete and glassblock. Nolan's Café soon followed suit, commissioning a handsome concrete art deco building to house its expanded restaurant facilities. Soon after, the Edina Recreation Center, complete with bowling alley, short-order café

The handsome Wooddale School, built at the edge of Edina's Country Club District, and, like the Morningside School built nearby on West 42nd Street at Grimes, one of two schools built in the mid-1920s to replace the aging Edina School in a time of rapid population growth in the village.

Edina Historical Society

A Sunday school class posed in front of the Cahill School, 1935.

Edina Historical Society

and beer license, went up on France Avenue around the corner from the movie theater.

Yet in the midst of these glamorous new buildings, through the years of the '30s, the feed store was still doing steady business, as was Lindquist's blacksmith shop, Thompson's Lumber Yard, and the creamery in a smaller form, reflecting the strong agricultural presence of the farmers in the southern districts of the village. The first telephone listings for Edina's downtown shops did not appear in directories until 1939. Just a few blocks out of the 'downtown' district, villagers and visitors could stop at farmhouses and roadside stands to buy berries and garden produce. West 51st Street did not exist west of France Avenue

South, only a long, winding private drive leading to the small farmhouse numbered 5048 France at the edge of the heavy woods that still ran north from the creekside. The woods themselves were home to a number of tramps—known only by their short names of Kent, Lamitz, Little Joe—who had fashioned year-round living quarters out of discarded crates, sod and tarpaper, recycled lumber, even an old milk wagon chassis.

The Schools and the Grange

The new suburbanites expected modern, high-quality schools, and conflict continued in Edina over the issue of school improvements long after Morningside's secession in 1920.

New elementary schools—Wooddale and Morningside—had been opened in both Morningside and Edina in the mid 1920s but the majority of Edina teens were still required to enroll in private schools or travel to Minneapolis' public high schools to finish their secondary education, a situation that would not change until Minneapolis raised its non-Minneapolis student tuition rate in 1941 and Edina found itself paying out a significant amount of tax money for some 300 Edina students enrolled in the Minneapolis system. Nevertheless, a citizen vote elected to continue to send students to other school systems rather than building inside their own village boundary.

The Minnehaha Grange hall remained in active use well into the war years, serving as the village council chambers until a new village hall was built in 1942. New members joined the Grange who were not in the farming industry: as Edina grew, so did the number of businesses in the community, which not only diversified the Grange membership but created new topics of interest, both social and cultural. In 1935 the Grange hall was moved east to Normandale Road to make way for construction of St. Stephen the Martyr Episcopal Church.

The Good Life in the '30s

While the Edina Country Club District would dominate village life from the mid-1920s

The Cameron Store on West 70th Street in the Cahill District, ca. 1940. The store served as Cahill's only garage, grocery, and gas station until after the Second World War, and had the only working telephone in the district for many years.

Edina Historical Society

Phyllis Morris, daughter of P.S. and Annette Morris of 4506 Moorland in the Country Club District, fishing at Minnehaha Creek. From the cover of the District's own monthly magazine *The Crier,* June 1936.

Edina Historical Society

every after, there were other estates and districts of affluence in the farther reaches of the village well beyond the commercial town center and the old mill crossroads. Some of these districts had been settled long ago; other districts bloomed in the years after the depression and represented a shift of the first Country Club District homebuyers to more pastoral settings at the edge of the village.

In the southwest of Edina, wooded hilltops were crowned with private hunting lodges overlooking Arrowhead and Indianhead Lakes. Not far to the east, on the site of the present-day Southdale Shopping Center, stood the Robinson-Day estate called "Oak Lodge." The park-like grounds and gardens that surrounded the great manor house were part of a 200-acre farm homesteaded shortly after the Civil War and eventually purchased by John Robinson, a pioneer lumberman, in 1880 for use as a hunting lodge. Deer, wolves and waterfowl were plentiful in the nearby woods and wetlands. Robinson's daughter converted Oak Lodge into a luxurious summer home at the turn of the century and brought in New York decorators to furnish the house, erecting white wooden fences along present-day France Avenue for a great distance to demarcate the property in the midst of farmlands. The estate endured until ground was broken for the Southdale Shopping Center in the early 1950s.

Far from the hunting lodges of the south

The golf links at the Interlachen Country Club in Edina's northwest district. The National Open was held at Interlachen in 1930.

Minnesota Historical Society

village districts, at the northwest corner of the village, lay Mirror Lake—a deep and long glacial pool of great loveliness and home to vast migrations of geese, ducks, egrets, cranes, and swans. Several great estate houses were built here overlooking the water meadows and connected by bridle paths, just nearby to the exclusive country club that gave its name 'Interlachen,' a Swiss word meaning 'between lakes,' to the district when it was built in 1911.

Interlachen Boulevard developed from a wagon track that ran straight west from the old Waterville Mill along the boundary fences of farmholdings out past Mirror Lake to Hopkins. It was in the 1930s that the Interlachen district developed to rival the Country Club District; indeed, first-time buyers in the Country Club District were later noted in the society news to have 'removed to Mirror Lake,' to Interlachen.

The exclusive nature of the district may have been presaged by the manner in which the six golfing partners wishing to leave the old Bryn Mawr Golf Club of Golden Valley in 1909 arrived with bags of gold at the door of the farmer holding the land they wished to purchase, expecting to persuade a country hayseed with the dazzling coinage. The farmer, no fool, declined to keep the gold in his house—though he was willing enough to sell the land, and the partners were required to return to Minneapolis where they reportedly sat up all

night guarding the gold with loaded shotguns until the banks opened in the morning.

Some truly sumptuous country estates were built at the north end of Mirror Lake. Among the finest of those early estates were "White Oaks" overlooking the lake above Interlachen Boulevard and "Pine Knoll " standing on present-day Schaefer Road. Built in 1936, Pine Knoll boasted an English-style manor house with a stone foundation and interior walnut paneling, servants quarters, a stable block with grooms' quarters, a barn, a summer cottage, a multi-bay garage with work-rooms, and several smaller out-buildings.

The Interlachen Country Club had garnered a national reputation early on, fostering the likes of Willie Kidd, Patty Berg, and Bobby Jones on William Watson's original 18-hole course, and hosting a multitude of celebrities over many years. In the 1930s the club was serving as the center for social activities in the district: Saturday nights were always formal club dances, Thursday nights were designated "maid's night off" for family suppers and Victrola parties, Sunday evenings were reserved for light tea suppers in acknowledgment of heavy Sunday after-church family dinners.

Lighthearted times such these were to last forever, or so it would seem in these mid-years of the 1930's. But stormclouds were on the horizon of Edina, of every village and city in the nation. By 1939 Hitler had invaded

Germany's neighbors and the Second World War had begun. The United States would withhold its armed forces for several more years but the effect of the war would be felt around the world. On December 7, 1941, following the bombing at Pearl Harbor, the United States entered the war and soon Americans were serving in military theaters both east and west.

World War II would be brought home to every family's doorstep.

The Hay & Stenson Liquor Store, 1936. This downtown Edina business stood on West 50th Street through the war years until its closing in 1948 after the village voted to control all liquor sales through municipal stores.

The Past

While the Edina Country Club District would dominate village life from the mid-1920s ever after, there were other estates and districts of significant affluence in the farther reaches of the village well beyond the commercial town center and the old mill crossroads...

Far from the hunting lodges of the south village districts, at the northwest corner of the village, lay Mirror Lake—a deep and long glacial pool of great loveliness and home to vast migrations of geese, ducks, egrets, cranes, and swans. Several great estate houses were built here on hilltops overlooking the water meadows and connected by bridle paths, just nearby to the exclusive country club that gave its name 'Interlachen,' a Swiss word meaning "between lakes," to the district when it was built in 1911.

Harold Schaefer at his estate 'Pine Knoll' at Mirror Lake in Edina's northwest district of Interlachen, ca. 1936.

Edina Historical Society

The Edina War Mothers, the Morningside Woman's Club, the Edina Garden Council, the Optimists Club, and the Edina Chapter of the American Red Cross (still noted as a "rural Hennepin County" chapter) combined forces with Edina's Minnehaha Grange to package supplies, sell war bonds, donate blood, raise money, establish canteens, and keep loving records of family and friends gone from the community in service overseas...

117

Edina's Minnehaha Grange No. 398, ca. 1945, at its long-time home at the intersection of Eden Avenue and Normandale Road (now Highway 100).

Edina Historical Society

HOME OF
MINNEHAHA GRANGE Nº 398
CHARTER 1873   ERECTED 1879

Red Cross volunteers gathered on the steps of Edina's Minnehaha Grange hall, 1942.

Edina Historical Society

Edina's volunteer fire department, 1942.

Edina Historical Society

The war came home to Edina as everywhere else in the nation. Building, development of any kind, came to a halt. Foodstuffs became rationed, store stock dwindled, services were retrenched. Gasoline was portioned out carefully, with city tanks being carefully monitored for emergency needs. The deep yards behind the bungalows in Morningside and Brookside evolved into Victory gardens, the eggs laid in backyard henhouses and the honey made in the hives under the fruit trees became a needed source of food. Vacant lots around the village center were turned over to community gardens and space apportioned to each family working the acreage. Edinans living around the 50th and France district who still had cows in backyard barns shared the milk supply.

In the Country Club District life changed little beyond the gathering of several families into single homes as enlistees went overseas. Gasoline rations were as applicable here as elsewhere, and many who were accustomed to automobile commuting walked north a half-mile to ride the Como-Harriet streetcar line along West 44th Street into Minneapolis.

In the Cahill District, at the south end of Edina, life was relatively unchanged by the war. Accustomed as they were to a simple and interdependent existence among family and neighbors, the Cahill farming families managed well despite the departure of fathers and brothers and sons into enlistment. What few

They Who Served

Images from the Minnehaha Grange Honor Roll Scrapbook: Mrs. Victor Irgens, Red Cross Chair (top left); Private John L. Duggan (lower left); Nancy Wallace West and friend, Women's Air Raid Defense, Hawaii (top right); Lt. Earl Horr (lower right).

Edina Historical Society

Regina Kelley's class at Cahill School, grades 1-6, at the end of World War II.

Edina Historical Society

area businesses existed endured, the one school-house and two churches continued to serve as vital community centers, and life went on.

At the northwest end of the village, at Interlachen, the war years saw large segments of the golf course turned over to Victory gardens and, as with the Country Club residents, businessmen accustomed to commuting to the city by automobile now left their vehicles idle in garages and rode the Hopkins streetcar line into town.

The Grange, a place of quiet activity for years, became newly prominent again in this increasingly suburban community. Supply drives of every kind were organized, often in coordination with the many civic and social

organizations that had bloomed in the village over the decades following the turn of the century: the Edina War Mothers, the Morningside Woman's Club, the Edina Garden Council, the Optimists Club, the Edina Chapter of the American Red Cross (still noted as a "rural Hennepin County" chapter), combined forces with Edina's Minnehaha Grange to package supplies, sell war bonds, donate blood, raise money, establish canteens, conserve precious supplies, and keep loving records of family and friends from the community in service overseas.

Edina men, and not a few women, of a great range of ages—seventeen to fifty—and occupations—virtually the gamut of Edina's professions, from farmer to corporate head—

An afternoon's fishing at Minnehaha Creek in the late 1930s.

Simplicity

In the Cahill District, at the south end of Edina, life was relatively unchanged by the war. Accustomed as they were to a simple and interdependent existence among family and neighbors, the Cahill farming families managed well despite the departure of fathers and brothers and sons into enlistment. What few area businesses existed endured, the one schoolhouse and two churches continued to serve as vital community centers, and life went on...

enlisted in the armed services and, one by one, left the village for overseas duty in the Navy, Army, Air Corps, Marine Corps, and special services—tank, medical, hospital, even the military railway service. At home, civil defense committees appointed wardens, home guard units were organized, and the city councillors drafted contingency crisis plans and ration programs for foodstuffs and fuel. Special attention was given to road maintenance, particularly in the wintertime, the memory of the 1941 Armistice Day snowstorm being not at all faded: Normandale Road (present-day Highway 100), the WPA's carefully landscaped 1930s roadway—locally named Lilac Way for the luxuriant growth of blooming bushes alongside the curbs—had been covered with snow over the rooflines of hundreds of stalled vehicles and life in the village had come to a complete halt for days. Now gasoline was stored against such recurrences and highway machinery was being obsessively maintained in the event of emergency need.

Community Life Goes On

The war years brought inevitable shifts to the local business community: Nolan's restaurant in downtown Edina had just built a new facility in 1941, appropriately named 'The Golf Terrace Café' and, though foodstuffs were not in abundance, the restaurant continued as a popular community gathering place to

The war years slowed business in Edina's commercial district, as with this service station on West 50th Street: gasoline and rubber were rationed, scrap metals gathered, foodstuffs apportioned. All village development came to a standstill in the early 1940s.

Memorial Day parade along West 50th Street en route to Edina's Grange hall, ca. 1943.

125

discuss the day's news and community activities. Hoyt's and the Brown Derby cafés, as with the Convention Grill up the road at Morningside's Westgate district, bravely printed business-as-usual menus—steaks, hotdishes, sandwiches, pastries, ice cream treats, sodas, coffee and tea—belying the inevitable daily problem of actually having the foodstuffs on hand to produce the requested menu items.

Some downtown businesses were sold to new owners, including Edina Realty, the France Avenue Beauty Salon, and the Town and Country Floral Shop, which was sold in 1941 to a long established local nursery called Bachman's. Some new businesses were established—several dentists opened offices in the

downtown intersection, a new Gambles store appeared as did the Edina Book Shop, the Brook-Haven Poultry Shop opened its doors, and a Pure Oil Station was built on the northwest corner of West 50th Street and Halifax (taking the place of a root beer stand). And, despite the scarcity of sugar and other baking supplies, no less than four new bakeries—Sweetart, Filipek, Mary Mac, and Heagles—opened for business in the village center in the early '40s.

Some interesting new products appeared at Nelson's Dry Goods, including nylon stockings, fifty cents a pair, a big hit with the village women because they were affordable and wouldn't run like the costlier silk stockings.

MILK BY THE GALLON

Larson's COUNTRY CREAM 35¢ QUART ALL PURPOSE

Larson's WHOLE MILK 34¢ GALLON CHECK THE CREAM LINE

HOVE'S SWEET CREAM BUTTER IN ROLLS · CARTONS · JARS

New Crop COMB HONEY 19¢ EXTRA HEAVY COMB

COMPETEN' SALESPEOP' TO SERVE YOU IN EVERY DEPARTME'

CANNED HAMS IN DELICATESSEN

Usinger's Genuine Milwaukee SAUSAGE

At Hove's Supermarket in the new Edina Shopping center, late 1940s. Postwar building got a fresh start in Edina with the rescinding of zoning regulations limiting the size of retail establishments in the village.

Edina Historical Society

Some businesses prided themselves on providing much needed entertainment for their community—the Edina and Westgate movie theaters played to busy weekend houses and the bowling lanes at the Edina Village (later 'Recreation') Center were popular.

Loss and Gain

Under Harold Stassen, an Edina native (and Grange member) who had been re-elected as Minnesota's governor in 1940, the first draftees and enlistees and many special units were called up from Minnesota after Pearl Harbor, and the National Guard was activated. Under Stassen, a Minnesota Defense Council was formed, as was a War Finance Committee and a State Postwar Council charged with planning the inevitable return to peacetime. In his re-election for a third term in 1942, Governor Stassen announced that, with the National Guard in service to the nation, he would organize and equip a Minnesota defense force. He also asked the legislature to fund postwar grants for all returning troops and for postwar reconstruction planning—highways, public buildings, and housing. One month before the adjournment of the legislature in 1943, Governor Stassen announced his intention to resign from state office (it would be his last elected post) for war service, entered the Navy, and served out the war as a flag officer under Admiral Halsey. The Minnehaha

CARE packages prepared for decimated European communities by Edina's Oakview Garden Club in the post-war years.

Edina Historical Society

Grange placed a photograph of their favorite son, in uniform and on deck of his ship, first in the Roll of Honor.

In all, some 304,000 Minnesota men and women went to war, of which more than 6,200 died in combat, of wounds, or from conditions of imprisonment. Edinans and Morningsiders suffered their share. Exhausted as they were by record crop production, vigilant rationing, and the willing turning-out of pockets to find another dollar to buy defense stamps, every effort was for their loved ones overseas, and the value of that effort was beyond measure even if their loss in kin was great. War memorial boards posted in both villages were visited day and night and the vigils became sources of solace and needed companionship.

Into the Postwar Era

The year of returning brought joyous homecomings, parades and celebrations, and the first efforts at a return to normal life. Minnesota's legislature bestowed cash bonuses to help the returnees get a fresh start, and the G.I. bill followed soon after to support a return to interrupted educations and careers.

Having come into the war with thoughtful management measures in place, Edina's government had survived the war with the need for only moderate belt-tightening, and there was sufficient funds on hand to renew

Grand Opening Day at Keller's Pharmacy in the new Edina Shopping Center, late 1940s.

Edina Historical Society

infrastructural work. A new form of government was instituted wherein an administrative manager for city services was appointed, foreshadowing the village's historic move to a council-manager form of government, the first in the state.

The end of the war was bringing a resurgence of development to all the first-tier suburbs around Minneapolis, and Edina's councillors saw the first indications of a population explosion. By the end of the first post-war year, countless developers were petitioning the village council with proposals for affordable housing for returning GI's and luxury developments for prosperous city dwellers ready to make the move to the fashionable suburbs. A new Planning Commission was established to take over the old Zoning Commission responsibilities: charged with much broader powers than its earlier incarnation, the new planning body sought limits to lot sizes and residential set-backs from property lines, ended the fashionable trend toward street cul-de-sacs, and amended a zoning ordinance to admit retail businesses larger than the long-approved "general store" model. And, after much heated debate, liquor stores were put under municipal control and restaurant liquor licenses were greatly reduced and regulated.

Within the Planning Commission's amended ordinances were the seeds of the greatest shift in Edina's character since Samuel Thorpe

The perfume counter, Keller's Drug Store, Edina Shopping Center. Keller's preceded Clancy's at the same location of West 50th Street and Halifax.

Edina Historical Society

Community

With the likes of the dashing new downtown shopping center, sporting everything a modern city needed (including a newfangled concept called a supermarket), Edina officials felt confident in saying that "the progressive building plan will furnish the community with a centralized and highly convenient modern civic and commercial hub equal to that of any community its size in the country...

KELLER'S SHADOW BOX

built the Country Club District: one year after the end of the war, plans for a multi-million dollar downtown shopping center were announced, intended to set a new modern standard in convenience, style, and service. No more would Edina be considered "rural Hennepin County" among philanthropic fundraisers and census takers. With the likes of the dashing new downtown shopping center, sporting everything a modern city needed (including a newfangled concept called a *supermarket)*, Edina officials felt confident in saying that "the progressive building plan will furnish the community with a centralized and highly convenient modern civic and commer-

cial hub equal to that of any community its size in the country."

How right they were, but none of the city's councillors could possibly know what waited in the wings for this stable, progressive, educated, well-to-do first-tier suburban American community: a totally enclosed, climate-controlled, multi-vendor retailing center, built in the midst of cornfields, the first in the nation, to be called "Southdale."

Chapter 10

*S*hopping centers are evolving, it's a new idea... I was born in Vienna, Austria, where I got my education in architecture. When I came to New York in 1939, I found that the migration of city dwellers to the suburbs was creating a new demand for shopping centers. I decided to pioneer this new field of architectural expression. We need a better term than 'shopping center.' At a center like Southdale...we have recreated an old architectural form—the square or plaza. There people may relax—not just shop."

Victor Gruen, Architect of Southdale Center
March 1954

131

Everything you needed—lunch, lingerie, and lipstick, cigars, sandals, and sodas, parakeets, perfumes, and potted plants, beachballs, bowties, and bathsalts— could be found at Woolworth's at the new Southdale Shopping Center.

Minnesota Historical Society

Raising the super structure (note the new
water tower already in place).

Edina Historical Society

Paving begins for the parking lots.

Edina Historical Society

Laying the Garden Court flooring.

Edina Historical Society

The Garden Court interior before the roofing
is installed.

Edina Historical Society

In 1952 the Dayton Development Company announced that a new retailing concept was coming to Minnesota: a fully enclosed, climate-controlled shopping mall to be called *Southdale*. It was to be built for $10 million, a staggering figure for the times, in a first-tier semi-rural suburb of Minneapolis called Edina.

Southdale Center was, at its conception and completion, history in the making: the retailing site at once constituted the largest shopping center in the world under one roof, the first shopping center in the world to provide total (versus partial) covered climate control of public areas, the first center in which two-level merchandising was combined with two-level parking, and the site of the largest indoor public area—the Garden Court—in the United States, 300 feet long, 110 feet wide, and fifty feet high.

Under One Roof

Mall is a word we all know well, use often. But in 1952 the concept of a collection of shops of that magnitude in a climate-controlled environment as proposed by the Dayton Development Company was a totally new plan, and it was going to happen in Minnesota, the Land of Long Winters where the idea of staying nicely warm while obtaining goods and services was a pleasing one.

Ground was broken for the new mall in 1954 on the site of the Day-Roberts farm, bounded by West 66th and 69th Streets between Xerxes and France Avenues.

Southdale Center Management

Edina was the first village in Minnesota to adopt a comprehensive zoning plan and such an approach to careful control over land development lent itself admirably to the process of consideration and approval of the Southdale proposal, which initially called for a 500-acre development to encompass a $7 million shopping center and a $3 million residential development. The actual shopping center construction would occupy eighty-four acres; an additional 400 acres was purchased to permit adjunct and compatible development. (Edina was not, interestingly, the Dayton brothers' first choice: economists hired to consider Daytons' expansion options made the initial recommendation in 1951 to build first in St. Paul and then begin to ring the Twin Cities with five or six suburban branches. Land in Woodbury and Bloomington was initially acquired only to be sold again later).

Donald C. Dayton, then president of The Dayton Company, would later say "The Southdale Center, Inc., will bring to this important area of greater Minneapolis an integrated, self-contained community. We are moving out to the perimeter of the community to accommodate the normal growth of the city, to make shopping and parking more convenient for the families in the suburbs. This is the first step in a long-range plan to give the Minneapolis metropolitan area several integrated shopping areas such as this." One year

Southdale Center nearing completion, August 1956.

Minnesota Historical Society

later, in 1953, Donaldson's Department Stores would agree with this concept, unnerving downtown Minneapolis retailers by electing to abandon plans for a new city center story and instead becoming co-anchor with Dayton's in the new Southdale mall.

Art and Architecture

The firm of Gruen & Associates, nationally-known architects for modern shopping developments, was selected to design the new retailing center. Victor Gruen considered the Southdale plan a "revolutionary concept" and stated that the development was "a preparation for the growth of the Twin Cities area." He was also to say that "the regional shopping center must, besides performing its commercial function, fill the vacuum created by the absence of social, cultural and civic crystallization points in our vast suburban areas." Gruen pointed to the factor of the automobile and its effect on suburban growth as a critical element in design for the new center.

Gruen's design as executed for the original building called for two-story single-store blocks anchoring opposite ends of the building, each containing a major department store. A series of smaller retail spaces, also block-shaped, would link the two larger masses. Retailers would be served by a unique underground delivery system. The smaller retail spaces were to cluster around an enclosed

Southdale's Garden Court was designed by architect Victor Gruen as a community special events site, a village square: this scene shows a fashion show in progress, ca. 1958.

Southdale Center Management

court rising a full two stories, with light made available from clerestory windows and skylights high above the court floor, a space to be heated in the winter, air-conditioned in the summer, and landscaped with plantings and walkways to give the illusion of being out-of-doors. "Since there are only 126 ideal shopping weather days," Gruen said, "we plan to make our own in Southdale...the center will be 'fair and mild' every day in the year."

The new shopping complex was elegant. The exterior was face with brick, granite and pre-cast concrete panels with a hard quartz finish, the interior walls showed decorative terra cotta tiles along the arcades and corridors. Imported Italian glass mosaic, white

Georgia marble, ceramic veneer with glazed design, mosaic fabricated stone, Vermont marble, terrazzo, Wisconsin sandstone, Swedish green marble, Italian ceramic tile with gold glaze, porcelain enamel window louvers, black walnut, oak stripping, Brazilian rosewood, and India teak graced many store interiors.

Gruen & Associates took the shopping center design to an entirely new level when they commissioned original artworks for Southdale Center. A massive metal "birdcage" sculpture was built to house fifty live birds, to the delight of countless children over the ensuing decades. A bronzed sculpture depicting children on stilts, a mosaic tile wall mural, and an abstract called "Golden Trees" on fifty-foot

vertical poles covered with bronze plates were also commissioned. So extraordinary was this choice that Gruen & Associates was invited to mount an exhibit entitled *Shopping Centers of Tomorrow* which opened to critical acclaim at Minneapolis' Walker Art Center in March 1954.

Groundbreaking ceremonies for Southdale Shopping Center took place in October 1954 in the cornfields of the Day-Roberts farm, bounded by the north-south arteries of France and Xerxes Avenues and the east-west routes of West 66th and West 69th Streets. Some 200,000 concrete blocks, 360,000 bricks, 15,000 square feet of marble, 24,000 square feet of glass, and 200 miles of electrical wiring were employed throughout the complex. Over

forty-three acres of parking lot were surfaced and a 440-foot well sunk to provide a required 1,500 gallon-per-minute water flow. The Center boasted a 10,000 kilowatt generator.

Southdale Shopping Center opened with an enormous public celebration on October 8, 1956. The project had taken just under five years to complete, with an estimated one million total hours invested in labor. The event was hailed in national architectural journals and in newspapers across the country and overseas. *Architectural Forum* declared Southdale Shopping Center to be one of the outstanding developments in the country. *The Minneapolis Tribune* ran daily notes on the interior details, including mention of imported

Southdale Center's parking lots, with night lighting designed by Westinghouse Electric, provided for five thousand automobiles. Shoppers found their cars by looking for the whimsical 'animal' signs designating specific parking areas.

Edina's police department inaugurated a new observation and apprehension technique which involved the use of a roof-top observer equipped with binoculars and portable radio communications to cars patrolling the area.

Edina Historical Society

Danish fixtures in the Egekvist Bakery store and a crystal chandelier in Donaldson's.

The Center garnered international architectural notice and drew developers, retailers, architects (including Frank Lloyd Wright, who was reportedly unimpressed), engineers, and diplomats from around the world to admire the new concept of multi-tiered environmentally controlled regional retailing. With service and maintenance facilities well hidden and parking areas charmingly marked with novel and colorful animal icons, the visitors knew they were seeing the future of shopping.

There was much to delight the eye and to please the shopper. The mall was home to two large department stores, eight women's clothing shops, five shoe stores, three men's and boy's clothing shops, a drug store, and many speciality retailers—millinery (hat), home furnishings, china, furs, pets, toys, jewelers, hardware, stationers, hobby and craft, florist, bakery, portrait studio, garden center—and was open three nights every week, an innovation for the convenience of customers. And the complex contained more than just retail goods: a post-office, shoe-repair shop, beauty and barber shops, bank, insurance agency, lost-and-found office, public restrooms, children's center and zoo were available in the basement (concourse) level. Shoppers went to Southdale for fashion shows, rock shows, auto shows, boat shows. Haircuts,

Woolworth's soda counter was a popular lunch spot in the first decades of Southdale Center.

Minnesota Historical Society

eyeglasses, shoe repair. They tried out mattresses, sat in soda fountain booths, hung out on mall benches. Bought tennis rackets, prom dresses, linens, and wedding bands, later baby clothes, bassinets, and bicycles.

Entertainments of every variety were provided in the Garden Court and parking lots by the Center public relations team: the Shrine Circus appeared (all of it!), as did the Minneapolis Symphony Orchestra, NASA exhibits, television broadcasts, and sports exhibitions. As the post-war baby-boomers moved into their early teens, their ideas of entertainment naturally changed: they shopped with friends, tested their buying strength (considerable), looked over other teens for social and fashion cues. So great were their numbers that they caused an entire reconsideration of retail marketing and Southdale Center became retailing's demographics grail.

That Southdale was built at all is a wonder. That it was built in Edina is, somehow, not surprising at all.

Chapter 11

*E*verybody just got along. You enjoyed people for who they were and it didn't particularly matter. I knew probably that our community was fairly well off, but I remember my grandfather always saying that the more you have, the more responsibility you have to share, to be responsible with what you have, to see that others are in need, to take part in your community, to put back into your community. I think both of my parents were good examples of doing that…"

Barbara Wehr Bergan, daughter of
Alfred and Elizabeth Wehr, Interview, 1998

141

Alfred Harrison Wehr and Elizabeth Ramsey Wood were married in 1940 and built their home in Edina's South Harriet Park neighborhood at the opening of World War II. Following the great change and upheaval of the war years, Al and Betty raised a family in Edina in the 1950s: their children became part of the American 'Baby Boom.'

Barbara Wehr Bergan / Paul Carson

Edina High School representatives to the 1965 Boys and Girls State, an intensive week-long mock government session held at the state capitol and attended by state high schools' top academic competitors. By the mid-1960s Edina had earned a reputation for the best secondary education program in Minnesota.

Edina Historical Society

The postwar years swept great fortune and great change into Edina's civic life. Educational and recreational programs begun in the 1950s took hold and bloomed, creating a magnet for city families. The postwar housing push, begun in the later 1940s, slackened slightly but not before creating entirely new residential districts in the village on both the west and south ends of the business district, and beginning the first major residential neighborhood construction boom in the Cahill district. The days of the isolated "village within a village" for Cahill were numbered.

Everywhere in Edina, elementary schools were in plan, churches were founded, and the village began its consideration of green space—parks and recreational facilities—for its citizens, not least for the pressure being brought to bear by developers to quickly consume the open land that remained in the village. Now the village council was challenged to consider what would best serve the community while trying at the same time to attract business and keep the tax base healthy.

A shift in the village's administrative structure, though not as a direct result of development pressures, took Edina to a new form of village government: the Council-Manager system. An earlier governance experiment in the mid-'40s had created the position of 'executive officer and manager,' an overseer to the village's fire, police and public works

Edina children learn the fundamentals of golf at the Braemar public links, ca. 1963. The Village of Edina created the extensive Braemar Park system in the southwest district of the village to ensure the availability of first-class public recreational facilities and programs for all its citizens.

Edina Historical Society

Groundbreaking ceremony on Wooddale Avenue, Colonial Church of Edina, ca. 1945. The Colonial Church, as with many of Edina's existing church communities, quickly outgrew its pre-war buildings. The Colonial Church would build yet again in southwestern Edina in the late 1970s, and expand those facilities in the mid-'80s.

Colonial Church of Edina

departments. The new Council-Manager structure created a check-and-balance approach for the village. It was immediately successful and set the pace once again as the first event of Council-Manager governance for Hennepin County municipalities, most of whom later adopted a similar approach.

Beyond the installation of a new system of governance, Edina had already been the first suburb in the county to construct a modern village hall (1954) and would go on to provide for fluoridated municipal drinking water (1956), appoint a full-time planning director (1957), secure Class A rating on municipal bonds (1962), and create a consolidated Public Safety program, bringing in police, fire and civil defense services (1963).

It was in the late 1950s and early 1960s that Edina made its final shift from rural to suburban life. The Country Club development and Morningside's needs had certainly hastened the process; now many of the remaining vestiges of the old agricultural community were disappearing: the feed store once located in Edina's downtown district had burned during the war, the mill was gone, rural electrification had come in with the New Deal, and the last passenger trip on Edina's north-south line of the Minneapolis, Northfield & Southern RRY (commonly known as the 'Dan Patch' line) had seen its last passenger trip in 1942.

VILLAGE OF EDINA

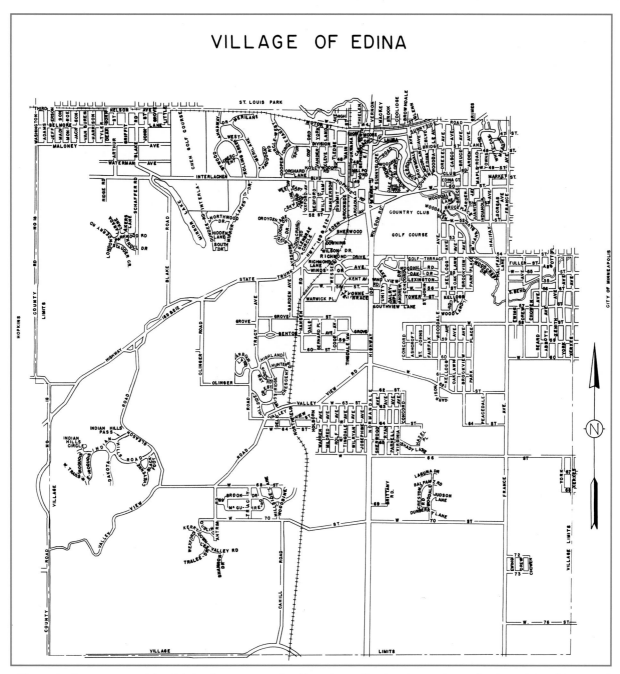

146

Village of Edina, 1952. Residential development remained largely confined to the northeast districts of the village until the 1960s when the freeway system was built around the boundaries of the village. It would not be until the late 1970s that the last farms would disappear in the southern Cahill district.

In 1950 less than 10,000 people lived in Edina, but by the late 1960s the population had reached 44,000, having doubled between 1950 and 1955, and doubled again by 1965. The pace of development in the village was being underscored by the pressure of getting "to and from" the city and soon the major arteries around and through the village were under siege for modernization. Even more, state plans were in the works by the late 1950s to implement a new metrowide 'Super Belt Line and Twin City Freeway System,' parts of which would cross Edina at the village midpoint and form a ribbon of concrete along the village's south and west perimeters. By the middle 1960s a greater part of the new system

had been built, inevitably displacing many of the villages oldest homesteads and farmsteads and drawing an ever-greater number of new suburban residents who could easily commute to work and shopping in the city.

Accommodating the children of the new residents in the village's educational system challenged and (literally) taxed the school budgets for much of the post-war decades. In 1930 the village had a total enrollment of only 680 students. By the late 1930s Edina schools were severely crowded, enough so that the village was sending over 300 students to schools in Minneapolis west and southwest districts. When the war ended, there was renewed acclaim for additional schools to be built. The

citizen votes carried for several more elementary programs and for a new high school. The first classes were enrolled at the Edina-Morningside Senior High School in 1949.

By the mid-'60s Edina had six elementary schools, two junior high schools, one high school, and three superb parochial schools—Our Lady of Grace, St. Peter's Lutheran, and Calvin Christian—with waiting lists to accommodate 10,100 children. Edina's reputation for scholastic excellence in its public schools became a state hallmark, and more families sought to live in the suburb in order to enroll their children in a now-famous school system: by 1960 it was estimated that over 80% of the village's high school graduates intended

to pursue a college education, a national phenomenon.

And there were other needs for the community's children: the village determined early on that recreation space would be a priority and that, in view of the rapidity of development, open land must be immediately purchased and held with city tax dollars for future playgrounds and parks. Soaring far beyond plans of even the most advanced village communities in the country, Edina conceived the Braemar Park plan in 1957, a comprehensive parklands acquisition and development program authorized by village voters approving a bond issue of $850,000. The magnificent Braemar park district, which contained multiple softball

Sonny Danens' horse-team digging out basements across the street from Al and Betty Wehr's corner house (under construction) on Alden and West 51st Street in Edina's new South Harriet Park, early 1940s. Post-war development boomed throughout northeast and central Edina and all along the eastern boundary with Minneapolis and Richfield.

Barbara Wehr Bergan / Paul Carson

The 1955 senior class officers of Edina-Morningside High School. The post-war boom years saw an acceleration of Edina's push for academic excellence and opportunity for all its children. Edina's high school students routinely took top state academic and athletic honors.

Edina Historical Society/New York Times

fields equipped for night games, a shooting range, a golf course, and an enclosed ice rink, came to occupy nearly one-twelfth of the (by now) very costly village land, in addition to the parklands already developed or in planning.

By 1965 the village had established no fewer than twenty-two neighborhood parks throughout the community, including some of the earliest municipal wetlands protection efforts in the county, backed by a full-scale program of organized recreational activities with expert supervised instruction in sports and crafts, an outdoor Olympic-scale competition swimming center, and a second public golf course. In 1965 the park system represented a village investment of over $1,100,000.

Morningside Returns

The 1960s brought more than just the roads and parks and schools: it brought Morningside back to the fold after almost fifty years of independence, a move of absolute necessity if the tiny district was to remain viable. In forty-six years of independence, Morningside had built a school, developed a popular commercial district, and successfully managed its affairs. Only in 1966, twelve years after the end of the streetcar operations and pressed on all sides by major urban and suburban communities, did Morningside return to the Edina fold and accept the benefits and challenges of being inside one of the county's most complicated and progressive cities. It

Downtown Edina in the
mid-1950s, looking west
along France Avenue from
West 50th Street.

Edina Historical Society

took many decades for Morningsiders, Edinans, and Minneapolitans to discard the new moniker "Edina-Morningside" and many long-time residents of Edina and southwest Minneapolis still call it by that name.

Morningside is greatly changed from its earliest years: the streetcar along which its lots were platted no longer runs, the handsome brick school that stood at West 42nd Street is gone now, torn down in 1977, and several of its hallmark businesses are now gone, most sadly the wonderful and historic Westgate Theater. But several venerable buildings—the Convention Grill and the Odd Fellows Hall— have seen thoughtful renewal and remain as busy commercial sites, and though there has

been an inevitable infill of modern housing along the old trolley right-of-way paralleling West 44th Street, the tree-shaded streets are still filled with the beautiful bungalow houses that are the signature of the district. Just a ways down the road, where Minnehaha Creek ties Morningside to Brookside, ducks still sail serenely down the waterway en route to the millpond, and deer make their way down the old Dan Patch rail bed towards the city parks.

The Future Meets the Past

In 1974, Edina officially became a City, a village no longer either in concept and in fact. Edina was now overwhelmingly built up for residential development and was facing new

Edina-Morningside High School commencement rehearsal, June 1955, taken by a *New York Times* journalism team as part of a profile on Edina's academic programs for the *NYT Sunday Magazine.* By the middle 1960s it was estimated that over eighty percent of the village's high school graduates intended to go on to college study, a national phenomenon.

Edina Historical Society/New York Times

pressures for commercial land usage but, overall, life was sweet in this first tier metropolitan suburb. Edina's school programs had achieved fame for excellence in the state and in the nation, the community athletics programs were providing every benefit of a healthful, active lifestyle available to children and adults alike, community participation in civic and social affairs was soaring, social services were an inalienable part of city life, neighborhood and government stability was rock solid.

Edina's growth in the postwar years was echoed by the rapid development of her neighbors—Richfield, Bloomington, Eden Prairie, St. Louis Park, and Hopkins—first- and second-tier suburbs experiencing the explosion of

single-family housing developed spurred by sympathetic federal policy and a staggering birth rate, the 'baby boom.' Nationwide, the migration from city to suburb was clear, documented, and dramatic.

In 1968 the Minnesota State Highway Department purchased the land on which the Grange hall stood and the Grange hall was moved to property owned by the Village of Edina and deeded as a living historical monument. The Grange, in turn, donated the building to the Village following refurbishing efforts, and the Village allowed the Grange to continue holding meetings in the building. Edina's Minnehaha Grange community was a mere shadow of the society's prime a century

ago, a reflection of the inevitable shift from a farming community to a sophisticated first-tier metropolitan suburb. There are a small handful of members in Edina gathered on an occasional basis, as they do still today, a fraternal and social organization conducting their meetings in the historic Grange hall. The hall itself was moved in the 1970s, at the request of Edina's newly formed Historic Preservation Commission (and one of Minnesota's first) to its present site at Tupa Historic Park on the southeast corner of West 50th Street and Highway 100 where it holds appropriate National Register status as an enduring symbol of village history.

Likewise, the one-room Cahill school, long

ago replaced by a modern elementary school building up the road in the rapidly developing south district, was also moved north at the request of Edina's Historic Preservation Commission to the Tupa Park site behind the city hall where it, too, was honored with National Register Status and lovingly restored to original condition. By the centennial year of 1888, the Cahill School had become Edina's most popular historic site visited by many hundreds of the city's school children of every year.

Village development quickened into the 1960s and the pace was sustained for more than twenty years afterwards. Interlachen's present-day development reflects the district's clear inheritance of the country estate, and

Morningside Elementary School, 1951. As with the Wooddale School near the Country Club District, this large educational facility on West 42nd Street was built to accommodate Edina-Morningside's "baby boom" children. The student population of the city declined dramatically after the late 1960s and, as was happening everywhere in the country, the decision was made to raze both buildings, Morningside in 1979, and Wooddale in 1985.

Edina Historical Society

remains one of Edina's wonderful secret corners. Most of the great estates were parceled and developed by the 1980s and today a new mode of executive mansion is rising on the remaining long-grazed stableyards and pasture lands. Much of the woodland that was home to deer, fox, and many species of birds is gone, and the increasing pressure of traffic along the busy roads encircling Interlachen challenges the City to maintain a pristine environment at Mirror Lake.

Elsewhere in the city, to the west and south of the commercial center at 50th and France, suburban development swept in and filled in right to city limits now well-defined by a ring of highways and freeways. The remaining farms vanished to be replaced by suburban ranch houses and townhomes. Thoughtfully, the city of Edina chose to honor the family farms that yielded land for suburban development by marking the old farm districts with street names reflecting the vicinity of family farmsteads, thus we find the familiar names of Browndale (Brown), Gleason (Gleeson), Grimes, McCauley, Tracy, Willson, Dewey Hill (Deweyhill), Cooper, Maloney, Hansen, Garrison, Roberts, Ryan, Duggan, Danens, Delaney, and Schaefer on residential street signs. Quite a few of the original farmhouses of the village remain in the present-day city well into the late 1980s, certainly the great National Register homes of the Bairds and the

Grimes families near Edina's downtown district, but also the Code, Hayes, Herret, Holman, Jones, Krake, Kyte, McNellis, Payne, Peterson, Schulz, Sly, and Wyman family homes, still to be found on their original sites. Though often altered and updated beyond recognition, several of these houses have their original barns still standing standing at the back of their lots amid their more modern neighbors.

The Country Club District has endured as Edina's premier residential district despite the development of magnificent new residential estate districts north at Interlachen (Rolling Green) and southwest (Indian Hills). The Country Club District represents an outstanding national example of architectural cohesion and planning and, as such, the entire District was accorded National Register Status in 1982. With the unhappy restrictive covenant now an historic document archived in the City files, the Country Club District has successfully demonstrated that Samuel Thorpe's vision of an ideal community—"a community where you can be proud to live, proud of your home...and of your neighbor's home as well"—could be an enduring reality. Now, as then, the District is home to a great number of women and men prominent in metropolitan and state business, industry, communications, financial services, and civic affairs.

Coaching baseball at Edina's Highland Field park, 1967. Edina's professional and volunteer Parks & Recreation staff combined to provide coaching for all of Edina's children free of charge. Girls as well as boys had equal access to sports training and facilities and Edina had the first girls competition hockey and softball teams in the region.

City of Edina

The Puppet Trailer was a creative and popular Edina Park and Recreation program, ca. 1959.

City of Edina

The Edina Mill, once sited at the edge of the Country Club District, was considered a terrible loss to city history: torn down in 1932, the old mill and tailrace have since been frequently memorialized in paintings and writings. The millpond remains a greatly treasured parkland in the midst of the city and the entire creek run through the city was developed for water recreation and hedged in with a greenway along both shores.

The original mill site was excavated by an archaeology team in the 1970s and, afterwards, an interpretive kiosk was erected to educate the public about the village's most vital resource of 150 years ago. Five of the original mill stones had long ago been placed throughout the city in commemoration: today, three stones are at the mill site as part of the historic park, a fourth millstone is in the floor of St. Stephen's Episcopal Church at Wooddale Avenue and West 50th Street, and the fifth is at the flagpole base at Our Lady of Grace Catholic Church on Normandale Road.

Far to the south of Morningside, the Southdale Shopping Center continues in its landmark status for the city. The Dayton Brothers' Southdale development was followed, as they had always planned, by other metro suburban 'Dales:' Rosedale, Brookdale, Ridgedale. Southdale's adjacent companion developments such as the Galleria have served to complement and support high-end retailing.

Other malls opened to compete around the metro region but none came even close to the 'Dales in scope or class until the old Met Sports Complex site in neighboring southeastern Bloomington gave way to an entirely new concept in commercial retailing, the Mall of America, now the largest such complex in the United States and drawing, as Southdale once did long ago, visitors, shoppers, and economic development representatives from around the world. Though Southdale has changed in appearance since its construction in 1954, and the sculptures, fishpond, aviary and basement zoo are gone, they are certainly not forgotten by the countless numbers of metro area shoppers who, in the 1950s, brought their buying power and their children to Southdale on Saturday afternoons.

That these two complexes—Southdale, still elegant and very busy with its success, and the Mall of America, standing stunningly large and handsome as a national retailing monument—should be in such close geographic proximity seems charmingly serendipitous and, at the same, entirely suitable, for in their shadows stand many precious and well-preserved historic structures—farmhouses, meetinghouses, schoolhouses—that remind us of what has always been true: that Edina, whether crossroads, village or city, has always been and will remain a progressive, vigorous, and enormously successful community.

The Edina-Morningside all-village baseball program enrolled hundreds of young people of all levels of skill into business-sponsored community teams. This is the Edina-Morningside Jaycees Senior Division, 1959.

Edina Park and Recreation hockey teams, 1960. Hockey (and later the high-skill European game of Bandy) was one of Edina's earliest and most popular programs. Complementing the school athletic programs, Edina's support for its Park and Recreation hockey programs have enabled city youth—boys and girls alike—to dominate state hockey competitions for forty years.

City of Edina

Sporting

By 1965 the village had established no fewer than twenty-two separate parks around the city backed by a full scale program of organized recreational activities with expert supervised instruction in sports and crafts, an outdoor Olympic-scale competition swimming center, and a second public golf course. In 1965 the park system represented the village's investment of $1,100,000...

Picking out the new skates, late 1950s.

Clearly, for Edina, the early patterns of thoughtful government and strong civic involvement has carried the city in excellent form into the post-war decades and through a prosperous passage beyond the city's centennial year of 1988, with every indication of sustaining in great good health far into the new millennium.

The Past

Edina, whether crossroads, village or city, has always been and remains a progressive, vigorous, and enormously successful community. Clearly…the early patterns of thoughtful government and strong civic involvement has carried Edina in excellent form through the post-war decades and through a prosperous passage well beyond the city's centennial year of 1988, with every indication of sustaining in great good health far into the new millennium…

Park and Recreation summer staff, ca. 1959. Edina's Park and Recreation staffing drew the best of the city's young adults. Competition for placement on summer Park and Rec staff groups was intense, and many who did find a place stayed on for careers of significant service to the city and to the community. Robert Kojetin (second row, second from left) only recently retired as Director of Edina's Park and Recreation programs. Kenneth Rosland (back row, right), then Assistant Parks Director, will retire in 1998 after eleven years as City Manager, forty-four years in all of service to the city.

City of Edina

National Register Properties in Edina

The Country Club District (First public sales 1924)
bounded by Sunnyside Road (N), Highway 100 (W),
West 50th Street (S), Arden Avenue (E)

The Grimes House (1869)
4200 West 44th Street

The Baird House (1886)
4400 West 50th Street

The Cahill School (1864)
Minnehaha Grange No. 398 (1879)
Tupa Historical Park, Eden Avenue at Highway 100

About the Author

Deborah Morse-Kahn, an historian and sociologist who served the Edina Historical Society as Archivist from 1992-1996, holds the Masters Degree in American Regional Studies. She specializes in research on the American Upper Midwest, particularly in the areas of historic preservation, immigration, ethnic and religious communities, the sociology of community, business history, and avocational archaeology. She consults and lectures frequently on area history and historic preservation processes and is a published author, having written in past years for *Minnesota Monthly, Corporate Report Minnesota,* the City of Edina's quarterly *About Town,* and Minneapolis' *Southwest Journal.*

Ms. Morse-Kahn served as Associate Editor and Research Director for the *Minnesota Business Almanac 1997-1998* (MSP Communications, Minneapolis) which won first prize in the Information Division of the 1998 Minnesota Book Awards. Her book *Last Journey of Henry David Thoreau* is in consideration for publication.

Ms. Morse-Kahn grew up at Lake Harriet and currently lives in the historic Minneapolis district of Linden Hills.

Research Notes

Material for this book was drawn from the archival manuscript, cartographic, and photographic collections, oral histories, and newspaper compilations of the Edina Historical Society, the Minnesota Historical Society, the Northwest Architectural Archives of the University of Minnesota, the Borchert Map Library of the University of Minnesota, the Hennepin History Center, the Minneapolis Collection of the Minneapolis Public Library, the Richfield Historical Society, the Bloomington Historical Society, the Eden Prairie Historical Society, the St. Louis Park Historical Society, the Hopkins Historical Society, the Western Hennepin County Pioneers Association, and from the departmental records of the City of Edina. Material used in this book from the author's unpublished manuscript *Last Journey of Henry David Thoreau* was found in the above archival collections and in the archives of the University of Wisconsin-Madison, Hamline University (Minnesota), the Spencer Natural History Collection and the 19th Century Collection of the Minneapolis Public Library, the Minnesota Horticultural Society, and the University of California-Santa Cruz.

The following publications were also consulted:

Atwater, Isaac and John H. Stevens, Editors, *History of Minneapolis and Hennepin County;* Munsell, 1895.

Blegen, Theodore C., *Minnesota: A History of the State (Second Edition);* St. Paul: Minnesota Historical Society, 1975 [1963].

Hesterman, Paul D., *From Settlement to Suburb: History of Edina, Minnesota;* Edina: Second Edition, 1993.

Holmquist, June Drenning, Editor, *They Chose Minnesota: A Survey of the State's Ethnic Groups;* St. Paul: Minnesota Historical Society, 1981.

Lanegran, David A. and Ernest R. Sandeen, *The Lake District of Minneapolis: A History of the Calhoun-Isles Community;* St. Paul: Living History Museum, 1979.

National Register of Historic Places: Minnesota Checklist; St. Paul: Minnesota Historical Society, 1998.

Neill, Edward Duffield, *History of Hennepin County and the City of Minneapolis;* North Star, 1881.

Scott, William W. and Jeffrey A. Hess, *History and Architecture of Edina, Minnesota;* Edina: City of Edina/Setter, Leach & Lindstrom Architects, 1988.

Swanson, Vern and Tom Clark, *From the Barber's Chair: 50th and France Avenue, 1936-1988;* Minneapolis: Nodin Press, 1988.

Survey: Historic Buildings of Edina, Minnesota; Edina: Heritage Preservation Board, City of Edina, 1979.

FOX MEADOW LN
HIDDEN LN
SOUTH DR
AYRSHIRE RD
LAKES
RD
PKWY
WAY
DUNCRAFT
GLENBRAE CIR
AYRSHIRE BLVD
VERNON
PINEWOOD TR
RICHWOOD DR
WINDSOR
HIGHLAND SCHOOL
EVANSWOOD LN
SCHOOL DISTRICT
PINE GROVE RD
HIGHWOOD DR W
BLAKE RD
PARKWOOD RD
IDLEWOOD LN
IDYLWOOD DR
DUNDEE
MIRROR
CHANTREY
GLENGARRY
MERRITT CIR
DONCASTER
GOYA LN
VERNON AVE
CANADIAN PACIFIC
W 56TH
KNOLL DR
SAXONY RD
PL
LESLEE LN
JEFFREY LN
DR W
HIGHWOOD DR
HEATHER LN
DUNDEE RD
HAWKES DR
TERR
TRACY AVE
RIDGE PARK RD
WARDEN AVE
PARK RD
57TH ST
CODE AV
HANSEN RD
AVE
PL
S. KNOLL DR
KAYMAR DR
EDEN PRAIRIE RD
WYCLIFFE
AVE
WARDEN
GROVE ST
DALE
BERNARD
CAMELBACK DR
VIEW LN
SCHAEFER RD
SCHAEFER CIR
VERNON AVE
BERNE CIR
BLAKE RIDGE RD
CT
GROVE CIR
MEROLD DR
RD
good samaritan methodist church
JOHNSON
OAK LN
GARDEN AVE
LYLE CIR
GROVE ST
BENTON AVE
SHERMAN CIR
OLINGER RD
AMY DR
STUART AVE
BENTON
COUNTRYSIDE DR
COUNTRYSIDE RD
COUNTRY-SIDE SCHOOL
OLINGER
SUN
OLINGER CIR
ARBOUR
HIGHLAND RD
HUNTER ST
WESTRIDGE
BIRCH CREST PARK
W 61S
BIRCHCRE
KILLARNEY LN
VIEW LN
SCHAEFER RD
GLACIER PL
61ST ST W
ARBOUR LN
TRACY
RIDGE
WAY RD
BLVD
CRESCENT
HANSEN
W 6
JEFF PL
CREST LA
DR
MADDOX
OLINGER BLVD
AVE
HILLSIDE
CRESCENT
VALLEY VIEW RD
COLONIAL CT
DARC LA
GLEASON CT
SANDPIPER CT
WAY
FIRE STATION
colonial church
TRACY
Jehovah Witness church
RD
WHITING
RED FOX CT
FALCON CT
PHEAS CT
CROSSTOWN HWY 62
CROSSTOWN HWY 62
LIMERICK LA
NORTHFIELD
64TH
DORON LA
DORON DR